Endorsements

Dream Beyond Yourself will challenge you to take a step of faith. The world says, "Ready, set, go." God usually says, "Go, set, ready." Sarah's life proves that as we are obedient to go, we can trust our God to prepare us for His mission.

Mark Batterson
New York Times best-selling
author of *The Circle Maker*
Lead Pastor of National Community Church

Dreams seem to be a dime a dozen these days, but a dream that is truly fought for, a dream that is made into a reality, is truly rare. In her book, *Dream Beyond Yourself,* Sarah challenges this generation not only to embrace a dream but to courageously step out in faith and live a life with an eternal destiny.

Jeanne Mayo
Founder and President of Youth Leader's Coach
International Speaker and Author

Sarah's book *Dream Beyond Yourself* offers a rare look into the real life of a missionary. Her transparency and open-hearted approach to this book is refreshing and will be helpful for any missional Christian trying to serve Jesus.

Gregory Beggs
Regional Director of Africa,
Assemblies of God World Missions

Just as the Holy Bible is relevant to all cultures and people groups, so too is *Dream Beyond Yourself.* This book is practical, highly inspirational, and easy to read. Sarah shares her powerful testimony while weaving in the truth of Scripture to challenge us to live a life of trust, availability, and obedience to God.

Dr. Gordon Lebelo
President of the International
Assemblies of God, South Africa

In *Dream Beyond Yourself,* Sarah reminds us that when our dream is bigger than us, God, the Dream-Giver, enables us to overcome life's challenges as we move forward in fulfilling His intended purpose for our lives.

John M. Palmer
President of EMERGE Counseling Services

As a teen, I devoured Christian biographies. Some were of well-known missionary heroes, others of the relatively unknown. They all shared one thing in common: the challenge to let Jesus be Lord of our lives and see what might happen. Sarah's story is both inspiring and utterly timely: to dare to live the dream—not our own, but God's. It's as counter-cultural as the gospel has always been and is undoubtedly the prophetic message for a global generation.

Colin Piper
Executive Director of the World Evangelical
Alliance Youth Commission

DREAM BEYOND YOURSELF

SARAH A. CAREINS

DREAM BEYOND YOURSELF

A Journey to Know God and Make God Known

Published by Author Academy Elite
P.O. Box 43, Powell, OH 43035
www.AuthorAcademyElite.com

Paperback ISBN-13: 978-1-64085-226-6
Hardcover ISBN-13: 978-1-64085-227-3
Library of Congress Control Number: 2018934018

Cover design: Danijela Mijailovic
Interior design: Jetlaunch.net

Dedication

To Mom and Dad
Thank you for always believing in God's dream
for me.

CONTENTS

FOREWORD   xi

INTRODUCTION: DREAM BEYOND YOURSELF   xiii

PART ONE: LEARN TO DREAM

1. THE MILKMAN (GOD'S DREAM)   3

2. SHYNESS OR FEAR? (GOD'S PREPARATION)   19

3. JUST AROUND THE CORNER
(GOD'S CONFIRMATION)   33

PART TWO: TRUST THE DREAM-GIVER

4. BEGGARS (GOD, MY PROVIDER)   53

5. STRIKE! (GOD, MY PEACE)   69

6. LADYBUGS (GOD, MY FATHER)   83

7. VAMPIRES (GOD, MY DEFENDER)   99

8. WARTS AND JAWBONES (GOD, MY HEALER)   115

PART THREE: SURRENDER YOUR DREAM

9. NEVER ALONE (DREAM TEAMS)   131

10. TRUE LOVE WAITED . . . AND WAITED . . . AND WAITED (DREAMS UNFULFILLED)   147

11. JUST WHEN YOU THOUGHT YOU'D FIGURED IT OUT . . . (DREAMS ON THE ALTAR)   163

12. THE BIG HOUSE (DREAMS FULFILLED)   177

EPILOGUE: DREAMS DO COME TRUE   195

ACKNOWLEDGMENTS   197

DISCUSSION QUESTIONS   199

ABOUT THE AUTHOR   217

ENDNOTES   219

FOREWORD

Dream Beyond Yourself is a breath of fresh air. It suggests that we need to make God the priority and leave behind the natural for the supernatural. Before we can chase a dream, we must identify and confess our excuses. *Dream Beyond Yourself* will motivate you to leave the excuses behind and start living God's dream for your life.

Sarah shares her incredible journey of transformation from a shy Indiana farm girl to a bold South African missionary. Though not all of us will move to a foreign country, Sarah encourages us to see that we all have a mission field, even in our backyards.

Each story will capture your attention and relate to your life. On this journey, Sarah shares how God will reveal Himself as our Provider, Peace, Father, Defender, and Healer. She reminds us that, as believers in Jesus, we are never alone. We are part of a greater team: the church.

Sarah is transparent as she shows us how to trust God with our unfulfilled dreams and love Him even more in the midst of disappointment. She takes us back to the ultimate truth that God's dream for people is to have a relationship with Jesus, live a transformed life, and share their faith with others.

This book is ideal not only for personal growth and study but also for small groups. Sarah's discussion questions are challenging and relevant for all ages and cultures.

Like Sarah, I've chosen to dream beyond myself. If you're not doing the same, maybe it's time to stop making excuses and dream beyond yourself too. Will you join us on the journey to know Him and make Him known?

Kary Oberbrunner
CEO of Redeem the Day and Igniting Souls
Author of *Elixir Project, Day Job to Dream Job,
The Deeper Path,* and *Your Secret Name.*

INTRODUCTION

DREAM BEYOND YOURSELF

"He must become greater; I must become less."
—John 3:30

Today's culture has become all about me. We take "selfies" and put our photos all over social media. When we dream of our futures, it's all about what we deserve or what we want. We want to become successful, even world-famous. Many have forgotten that God has a dream for our lives. He has a plan. Shouldn't our aim be "less of me and more of God?"

Don't get me wrong; I have personal dreams for my life. As I write this, I'm 33 years old and still single. I want to get married and have children. However, that dream has not happened for me yet. I've also longed to go to the top of the Eiffel Tower in Paris, visit the Roman Coliseum, and walk in the mist of Victoria Falls, one of the Seven Natural Wonders of the World.

Amazingly, I've experienced all those things, yet other dreams remain unfulfilled.

"Take delight in the Lord, and he will give you the desires of your heart" (Psalm 37:4). If I delight in God's dreams, His desires will become my desires. His dreams will become my dreams.

We should fill our lives with more than our personal dreams. We must learn to dream beyond ourselves. Ask yourself this: does your personal vision impact God's Kingdom? Will it touch future generations? Your life will find more purpose when you begin to dream beyond yourself.

The Apostle Paul, formerly called Saul, thought he was fighting for God's dream and protecting the religious system of his day. In actuality, he was fighting against God.

"As he neared Damascus on his journey, suddenly a light from heaven flashed around him. He fell to the ground and heard a voice say to him, "Saul, Saul, why do you persecute me?" (Acts 9:3–4).

Sometimes we need a Damascus road experience where God hits us with the light of His truth, and we fall to our knees. We need an encounter with Jesus to get us on the right path.

By the standards of the day, Saul was a success. The religious leaders respected and even encouraged his actions. Saul thought he was doing good, but in truth, he was persecuting true believers. Accomplishing "good" dreams does not mean we are fulfilling God's dreams.

A God Dream always leads to the salvation of others. God's Dream was for Saul to spread the truth of Jesus, not prevent it. Dreaming "beyond ourselves" involves us looking beyond our own lives and seeing how we can impact others.

Some people may not understand how God could use someone like you. What people don't see is that it's not about you. It's about God. Don't let fear stop you. Don't disqualify yourself. God will use anyone who is willing and obedient.

The Lord told a man named Ananias to go pray for Saul. However, Ananias was afraid that Saul was still his old self. When Ananias questioned God about using Saul, God replied, "This man is my chosen instrument to carry my name before the Gentiles and their kings and before the people of Israel. . . ." Then Ananias obeyed God and prayed for him. Saul's sight was restored, and he was filled with the Holy Spirit (Acts 9:15–18).

Like Paul and Ananias, you are God's chosen instrument to fulfill His dream of reaching lost people. Let today be your Damascus road moment. The Lord will give you new vision and equip you with His Holy Spirit. God will fulfill His calling for your life if you will trust and obey Him.

This dream will involve surrender and sacrifice. Saul used to persecute believers. Now he would be persecuted. He would suffer much for the name of Jesus (Acts 9:16). Like Saul, we must learn to walk in God's dream despite the cost.

Saul would later change his Jewish name to his Roman name, Paul. His ministry to the Gentiles may be the reason he wanted to go by his Roman name, or maybe he didn't want to be associated with his past. My point is that his new name also held a new meaning. The name Paul means "little." Every time someone said "Paul," it reminded him that he was "the little one" and God was "the big one."

God wants you to love Him more than any dream you have. As you begin to dream beyond yourself, know that God's vision for your life is exactly what you would choose if you knew all the facts. He sees the big picture. We only see a small piece of the puzzle.

Trust that God's dream is the best one for your life. He longs to take you on a grand adventure with Him. His dream is to walk with you on your journey to knowing Him and making Him known to the world.

PART ONE
LEARN TO DREAM

CHAPTER ONE:
THE MILKMAN (GOD'S DREAM)

"... so that all the peoples of the earth may know that the Lord is God and that there is no other."
—1 Kings 8:60

Are Your Dreams God's Dreams?

A dream is a goal, ambition, or hope.

A "God dream" is God's perfect will. God is not a man that He would fall asleep (Psalm 121:3). His dreams are not just a wish. A God dream is His perfect plan that becomes your passion when united with His heart.

Part of God's dream included Jesus coming to this earth to die on the cross for our sins. Jesus paid the penalty for our sin so we wouldn't have to. God's plan did not end on the cross. It included Jesus being raised from the dead and sending the Holy Spirit to be with us.

God's dream is for us to be forgiven and saved from eternal punishment.

God's dream is for us to share Jesus with those who have not heard of Him.

God's dream is for everyone to spend eternity with Him in Heaven and have a personal relationship with Him while we are here on earth.

If you have a relationship with Jesus Christ today, then part of God's plan has already been accomplished in your life. However, God's dream includes more people than you alone. God wants to make sure that everyone has at least been given the opportunity to accept or reject Him.

Sometimes the fulfillment of this dream comes through a testimony.

What's your testimony?

Everyone has a testimony.

If you were in a courtroom, a testimony would be defined as the spoken word that recounts the evidence or proof of the existence of something in your life. If you were in church, it would be the evidence of the existence of God in your life. Whether you realize it or not, we all have a testimony of the existence of God in our lives.

I grew up in a small church where testimony time was a regular occurrence. There were "cool" testimonies like people coming out of drug abuse. Then there were "boring" testimonies—the ones where the person went on and on and made no sense.

For the longest time, I did not believe I had a testimony. I am not perfect, but I never did drugs or made my parents go (too) crazy. In fact, for as long as I can remember, I have loved Jesus and desired a relationship with Him. What I didn't realize was that this was my testimony. Because Jesus was in my life, He kept me away from drugs and bad relationships. I did not need a "cool" story.

Jesus never did drugs, yet this man changed the world. Sometimes culture makes you believe you had to have "been there" to help someone. Yes, that understanding can help you relate, and God can use your past for His glory, but He can also use your lack of a past. People listened to what Jesus had to say because He had the testimony of knowing the Father. Because of the evidence of a relationship with Jesus in my life, I have a testimony. And so do you. I pray that you do know Jesus. If not, let this be the beginning of a beautiful relationship.

> People listened to what Jesus had to say because He had the testimony of knowing the Father.

My love for God would never have been possible if it were not for my parents providing the opportunity. The legacy that our parents give us includes their testimony—good or bad. If they lived well, will you choose to take it to another level? If your parents were messed up, will you make the pain stop with you? What legacy will you leave for future generations?

Set up by the Milkman

When my parents married in 1980, society still had a sense of right and wrong. My parents were both struggling with sin; my mom was not a virgin, and my dad was addicted to pornography. My mom felt conviction for her lifestyle. She told God that she would not continue dating, and the next guy she met would have to be the "one."

Her father constantly pressured her to find a husband. They lived on a small Indiana dairy farm, so he enlisted the help of the milkman to set up his daughter with blind dates.

My mom's next date happened to be my father. Only four months after meeting each other, my parents married. (The milkman was the best man at their wedding—seriously.) My dad was almost 20 years old and my mom was 23. Soon after the wedding bells rang, they had my sister, Jennifer, in 1981. I came along a couple of years after that, in 1983. Then in 1986, my mom became pregnant again. To her dismay, my unborn sibling's life ended in a miscarriage.

The miscarriage was the turning point. Confused and broken, my mom felt this loss so greatly that it made her think long and hard about her relationship with God. She became frustrated with religion and began to seek something deeper. There had to be more to God than just attending a church on Sunday. I vaguely remember visiting a lot of churches in this search for truth. Eventually, we found a small Assemblies of God church on the southwest side of Fort Wayne, Indiana.

The loss of the baby also affected my father. With some convincing from my mother, my dad also started to attend the Assemblies of God church. On the way home after each service, he would say to her, "Did you tell the pastor something? He is talking about me."

It was not long before my dad, under the Holy Spirit's conviction, confessed to my mom all that he had been doing. My mother had known her marriage was not perfect, but she had been clueless about most of my father's struggles. All she could do was look out the window and pray, "Jesus, what am I going to do?" At that moment, she felt Jesus' presence come into the room, and His power helped her through the days ahead.

One evening soon after Dad's confession, he was still not home from work although it was way past his usual hour. After tucking us children into bed, Mom spent hours on her knees praying for my father. When he finally arrived home, he told her of the hopelessness he felt. With tears flowing down his cheeks, he explained that it had taken everything in him to keep from driving the truck into a tree to kill himself. Shaken and desperate, he agreed to call the pastor.

Around midnight, the pastor arrived and didn't leave until long after one o'clock in the morning. Despite the late hour, he took the time to pray with my father. This night was the beginning of a spiritual transformation.

Over the next few years, my brothers, Andy (1987) and Chad (1989), were born. Our church also got a new pastor, Troy Trout. Pastor Troy and his wife Teresa played a huge role in discipling my parents. They also had an incredible vision to reach the children of the community. Every Wednesday night, my father helped drive the church bus to pick up unchurched kids.

Pastor Troy and Teresa's ministry to children made a huge impact on my life and helped build a solid foundation of faith. I still remember Pastor Troy teaching us about Jonah and the big fish. My father dressed up like Jonah and ran into the church with seaweed all over him! Another time, the pastor taught about Peter walking on water with a small kiddie pool filled with water. A few children were allowed to test it and see if they could also walk on water. Every story taught me to have faith in a God who loved me very much.

By the time I was almost seven years old, I had decided to make my faith public. Pastor Troy baptized me in a dirty pond just down the road from my childhood home. God's dream was beginning to come true for my life.

All of our experiences are the building blocks of life. God has a dream for our lives. We can choose to make our experiences a staircase to God's dream, sit on the blocks of life, or even be crushed by them.

We all have to leave our pasts and move forward. Looking at old family photos, I see a physical difference in my father after he committed his life to Christ. He wasn't perfect and still makes mistakes, but he chose to seek God and lay his sins at Jesus' feet. When we change the inside of our heart, it will also flow outward to our daily lives.

But our salvation is not the end of the journey. Many of the testimonies people share at church tend to be from 20 years ago. A testimony is not only how we met Jesus but also what He is currently doing in our lives. The truth is that our salvation is only the beginning of God's dream.

A Heart for Missions

Jesus told us to "go and make disciples of all nations" (Matthew 28:19). There are many more people in the world who still need to hear the message of Jesus. It is up to us to share with them how we met God and how He has changed our lives.

This desire to reach the world led Pastor Troy and his family to leave our church. They embarked on a new season of life to serve as missionaries in Guinea-Bissau, West Africa, and later the Cape Verde Islands. This was my first exposure to missions. Teresa Trout and my mom would often write letters back and forth. (It was the 1990s, and hand-written letters were still a form of communication.)

As a child, I always loved checking our mailbox because a letter from Africa might be waiting for us.

Every photo and story captivated my attention. On a few special occasions, we even received more than a letter, i.e. the currency of Guinea-Bissau and an African dress. Whenever I had to write a report on a foreign country in school, I always requested Guinea-Bissau because I felt privileged to have "inside information." If a speech were needed, I would try to impress the teacher and the class by wearing a real African dress and passing around the currency for everyone to see.

But is everyone a "missionary"?

A missionary is a "sent one." In churches today, it seems that everyone is called a "missionary." We are all on a mission to accomplish the Great Commission. All of us are called to make disciples. We are all called to be witnesses of our faith. However, not everyone is actually ready to sacrifice. Not everyone is willing to leave the country of their birth and go to a foreign land. One of the most courageous things a person can do is to sacrifice their short time on earth with their own family so that others can be with their families for all eternity.

Because of their sacrifice, missionaries who go to foreign lands have always been my biggest heroes. Whenever missionaries came to visit our church, I sat on the edge of my pew and listened attentively. I loved hearing stories of the power of God moving around the world. While other children were collecting baseball cards, I was collecting missionary prayer cards. Instead of a card with a celebrity's photo, there was an average family picture next to the words "Missionaries to India." My goal was to collect as many countries as possible and consistently pray for each missionary.

God began working on me early, growing my heart for missions and different people groups. Indiana farming communities are rarely diverse. The demographic of my elementary school was primarily "white" students. I only remember maybe two or three students who did not have white skin. When I was in fifth grade, my best friend's family adopted two sisters from Vietnam, a country in Southeast Asia, who were also close to my age. Since they were part of my best friend's family, they also became my friends. The stories of their childhood in Vietnam fascinated me. I loved their uniqueness. I loved them.

One year for Christmas, I asked my mom for a certain kind of baby doll. It was called a "water baby." It was made of soft plastic and could be filled with hot water to make the baby feel real—heavy and warm. When she went to the store, there were no white water babies left, so she ended up buying me a black water baby. This doll became my favorite. Her name was "Katie," and I took her everywhere I went. In fact, I still have her safely tucked away at my parents' home.

Since that Christmas, I never wanted white dolls again. I always asked for African or "chocolate" babies. God was growing my heart for the African people, even in a "white" society. God was teaching me that His dream is to reach *all* people—*all* tribes and nations.

Jesus loves all the little children of the world—red, yellow, black, and white.

God's dream was becoming my dream. Is it becoming yours?

A Gift

Jesus knew that we could not live a missional life without assistance. God gave us the gift of the Holy Spirit so that we could share our testimonies and live our lives with boldness. The purpose of the Holy Spirit is to empower us as witnesses to our communities, regions, and even the world (Acts 1:8). If the disciples of Jesus' day needed the Holy Spirit, how much more do we need the Spirit today?

Peter, one of the twelve disciples of Jesus, was a man who made a lot of mistakes. When the disciples were out in a boat in the middle of a storm, Peter had enough faith to get out and walk on water toward Jesus. But then he doubted and began to sink. In Jesus' last moments before the cross, when Peter was supposed to be praying with Jesus in the Garden of Gethsemane, Peter was dreaming in his sleep. His final major failure came when Jesus was being led to the cross; Peter denied even knowing Jesus three times.

There is a change in Peter that takes place in Acts 2. Before Jesus ascended into Heaven, He told the disciples to "wait for the gift my Father promised" (Acts 1:4). This led about 120 believers to seek God and wait for this gift. After 10 days of waiting and praying, "all of them were filled with the Holy Spirit and began to speak in other tongues as the Spirit enabled them" (Acts 2:4). Then Peter stood up to speak to the crowd.

"In the last days, God says, I will pour out my Spirit on all people. Your sons and daughters will prophesy, your young men will see visions, your old men will dream dreams. Even on my servants, both men and women, I will pour out my Spirit in those days, and they will prophesy.

"And everyone who calls on the name of the Lord will be saved.

"Repent and be baptized, every one of you, in the name of Jesus Christ for the forgiveness of your sins. And you will receive the gift of the Holy Spirit. The promise is for you and your children and for all who are far off—for all whom the Lord our God will call."

With many other words he warned them; and he pleaded with them, "Save yourselves from this corrupt generation." Those who accepted his message were baptized, and about three thousand were added to their number that day (Acts 2:17–18, 21, 38b–41).

Three thousand people were saved at Peter's first sermon! Peter no longer walked in fear—he walked in faith. He emphasized that the Holy Spirit is for young and old, men and women—*all* people. This wasn't just something for the disciples' day but for all who were far off, all whom the Lord would call. He has called you. The gift of the Holy Spirit is also for today's believers.

The Holy Spirit is a gift. Most children ask for their Christmas presents in advance and even make a list for their parents or Santa Claus. Then on Christmas day, they joyfully run out of their bedrooms to the Christmas tree to receive them. They tear open each gift in anticipation of the good gift their parent or Father Christmas has given them. The child didn't have to do anything to get the gift. It was given because their mother and father loved them.

If you haven't yet experienced the gift of the Holy Spirit, ask your heavenly Father, and He will give it to you. If you have asked and not received, then keep asking because it is a promise from God.

If you then, though you are evil, know how to give good gifts to your children, how much more will your Father in heaven give the Holy Spirit to those who ask him! (Luke 11:13).

A week before my tenth birthday, our church held a series of "revival" services. There was a special guest speaker, and people came expecting God to do something in their lives. Before leaving our home for church,

I told my mom, "Tonight I'm going to be baptized in the Holy Spirit."

I spent about an hour at the altar earnestly seeking God. Others may have given up after a few minutes, but I was not going to leave until I'd received what was promised from God. At last, with stammering lips, I began to speak in tongues. Oh, the faith of a child!

After that experience, I wanted to read the entire Bible. The book of Acts was my favorite as it held the stories of the first missionaries. I hung Scripture verses all over the walls of my side of the bedroom that I shared with my sister. My hunger for the Lord grew deeper. Even childhood fights with my sister would end with me closing our bedroom door and praying in tongues. My sister could not fight with that!

When we are born again, we receive a deposit of the Holy Spirit in our lives. Every believer is a temple of the Holy Spirit. Just as you fill a cup with water, the Spirit dwells in you at salvation. However, the Baptism of the Holy Spirit is a separate occurrence. This cup of water is now immersed in the water source. The water is no longer just inside your cup; it flows out of your cup to impact others.

When you are baptized in the Holy Spirit, you will get other people "wet."

The Baptism in the Holy Spirit helps you to dream beyond yourself. Salvation put the Holy Spirit in you, now the Baptism of the Holy Spirit will bring the Spirit out of you to touch others.

"Did you receive the Holy Spirit when you believed?" They answered, "No, we have not even heard that

there is a Holy Spirit. . . ." When Paul placed his hands on them, the Holy Spirit came on them, and they spoke in tongues and prophesied (Acts 19:2b, 6).

The evidence that you have been baptized is that you will begin to speak in a language that you do not understand. It can be a language of the angels or of this earth not known to you. This is called speaking in tongues.

Paul says that he "speaks in tongues more than all of you" (1 Corinthians 14:18). Here he is referring to our prayer language. God calls every believer to seek a private prayer language and "pray in the Spirit" (Ephesians 6:18). There is also a gift of tongues for public worship. The public gift must be interpreted so that everyone can understand. God gives each believer different spiritual gifts for public use, but a private prayer language is available to all who seek it (see 1 Corinthians, chapters 12 and 14).

It is interesting that God uses the tongue as the evidence that we have been baptized in the Holy Spirit. Our faith has to allow God's heavenly language to be spoken from our own mouths. God never takes hold of your tongue. You have to initiate with your own will. You can start speaking in tongues, and you can choose to stop. You are in control of your body (1 Corinthians 14:32). We must speak out our prayer language in faith.

The same is true of sharing your testimony or witnessing to lost people. You must take a step of faith to go and talk to them. You may not know what you are going to say, but at the moment you need to speak, God will put the words in your mouth.

The Baptism in the Holy Spirit is given to us so that we will witness. When you witness to someone, you have to speak in a language they understand. You have to walk up to them in faith and believe that God will give you words. The Holy Spirit guides you and empowers you.

If you are not willing to witness to others, why would God pour out His Holy Spirit on you? God promises that this gift is for all believers. He won't force His gift upon you. You must reach out and receive it in faith.

Prayer

After I had received the Baptism in the Holy Spirit, prayer became one of my passions. Every Monday evening, I would hurry to finish my schoolwork so I could join my mom at the church prayer meetings. Only a few dedicated people attended. I was usually the only young person, but this did not discourage me. As I heard others pray out loud, my own voice began to grow louder. My desire to spend time with God increased as the presence of the Lord met me every Monday night.

From grade seven until I graduated from high school, every morning before the school bell rang, some other students and I would gather to pray. Praise God for my middle school choir teacher and our high school math teacher! They allowed us to use their classrooms as prayer rooms before our public school day began. Sometimes several students were there; other times it was only one other girl and myself. We faithfully joined together to pray for our classmates, teachers, and the administration.

Whenever we pray, we reach God's heart. Our eyes begin to see others as God sees them, and our hearts break for what breaks God's heart. When we pray in the Spirit, we pray in alignment with God's will or dream for our lives. Even when we don't know what to pray, the Holy Spirit will pray on our behalf (Romans 8:26).

"Called" to What?

The story of Jesus' childhood has caught my attention over the years. I find it interesting that Jesus was 12 years old when He knew He needed to be "about his Father's business" (Luke 2:49, NKJV).

When I was 12 years old, my family and I attended a church family camp in Hartford City, Indiana. During one of the evening services, the presence of the Holy Spirit surrounded me so strongly that I fell to my knees and tears fell from my eyes. At that moment, I somehow knew God was asking me to give my life to full-time ministry. There was no audible voice from Heaven—only a heavy burden and impression on my heart.

Back in our camper after the service, my mom tried to comfort me. This calling was confusing. At 12, I thought God told you the details like "be a missionary" or "be a youth pastor." The only detail I heard was "ministry," with no specifics.

Now I realize that God only tells you what you need to know when you need to know it. If He had told me then what I know now, I probably would have been too afraid to take the first step. Baby steps are the graceful way God has dealt with my journey so far.

"Trust in the Lord with all your heart and lean not on your own understanding; in all your ways submit to him, and he will make your paths straight" (Proverbs 3:5–6).

God gives us just enough light for each step. He shines His light on the part of the path we need to travel. He often takes us step-by-step or moment-by-moment.

God had saved me. He had filled me with the Holy Spirit. Now He was calling me to take steps of faith to reach the unsaved.

A Willing Heart

Despite my hunger for God and deep desire to serve Him, I remained a very shy and awkward girl throughout middle school and high school. Most of this time, I had braces on my teeth and an out-of-style haircut. My goal was to hide in the background and not be noticed. My social status would probably be called "nerd." In eighth grade, when the teachers gave awards at the end of the semester, I was awarded "the quietest award." If I'd been a superhero, my superpower would have been "silence."

Yes, I prayed at school, but I never shared my faith boldly with those students who needed Christ. I was baptized in the Holy Spirit, but I was not allowing the Spirit to speak through me as a bold witness for Christ. Witnessing was something that I knew I should do and I prayed that I would, but my shyness was an obstacle.

When I finally graduated, I wondered if any of the other students had even known that I'd existed over the past four years of high school. I was an excellent student graduating with distinction and was ranked fifth out of 202 students. I found my self-worth in the praise I received for my good grades. I would later realize how grades could become a false "god."

The truth is that our grades, or any form of earthly praise, will not go to Heaven with us. The only thing we can take to Heaven is other people. Being a good student is not wrong, but sometimes we have to look up from the books and share Jesus with those next to us.

During high school, the question loomed: "What will you do when you graduate?"

My excellent grades could have given me scholarships to attend any university or college of my choice. But my calling to ministry was still very real to me. I wanted to be used by God.

I recognized that my shyness was holding me back. I no longer wanted to hide in the crowds. I wanted God to amplify my voice.

Here is a poem that I cut out from Focus on the Family's *Brio* magazine. It hung in my room for several years:

A Willing Heart

I may be young right now,
But I know God's going to use me somehow.
I may be quiet and I may be shy,
But my little voice God will amplify.
I may not know much about God,
But every day I'm learning more about His love.
I may not be the most powerful girl,
But God needs me to reach this world.
You may wonder why God would use
someone as young as me,
If you would ask God, He'd say, "Because she's willing."
—Lorie Elmore, 15 years old,
from Huntington, Arkansas

This was my hope and became my prayer. This dream was the beginning of my journey to know God more and make God known.

God's dream was becoming my dream. The dream was beyond me. It would take the supernatural power of the Holy Spirit to accomplish it.

The evidence of God in my life, especially throughout my childhood, is undeniable. Look carefully into your own life. Do you see evidence of God?

What is holding you back from God's dream for your life? What steps will you take to move past your excuses?

The journey is not over. It is just beginning. Take a step of faith.

CHAPTER TWO:
SHYNESS OR FEAR? (GOD'S PREPARATION)

"For God has not given us a spirit of fear, but of power and of love and of a sound mind."
—2 Timothy 1:7 (NKJV)

God doesn't call the equipped. He equips the called.

It's not a question of whether or not you are "called." Every believer is called to be a witness. Whether you are a pastor, missionary, or just a regular believer, you are called to "go and make disciples."

In the book of Genesis, God gave Joseph His dream for his life. There were probably moments when Joseph wondered if God had forgotten the dream. He was betrayed by his brothers, thrown into a pit, sold as a slave, locked in a prison, and forgotten by his friends. However, each part of his journey prepared him for the palace. He grew in leadership—from being in charge of Potiphar's house to taking care of the prison. Each transition readied him to lead Egypt as second-in-command.

Joseph would later tell his brothers, "You intended to harm me, but God intended it for good to accomplish what is now being done, the saving of many lives" (Genesis 50:20).

Sometimes our journey to the dream doesn't look glamorous. It may involve a few pits and even a prison before you ever reach a palace.

> **If God gave us the dream without character, the dream would fall apart.**

Every step of the journey is building our character. If God gave us the dream without character, the dream would fall apart. He first prepares us and conditions us to be strong enough to hold onto the life He calls us to.

> *Brothers, think of what you were when you were called. Not many of you were wise by human standards; not many were influential; not many were of noble birth. But God chose the foolish things of the world to shame the wise; God chose the weak things of the world to shame the strong. He chose the lowly things of the world and the despised things—and the things that are not—to nullify the things that are, so that no one may boast before him. . . . Let him who boasts boast in the Lord (1 Corinthians 1:26–29, 31b).*

When I was called, I was so weak and foolish. I can boast only in the Lord! Those who knew me in my childhood and teen years can testify to how God has transformed me from a shy girl to a bold witness for Christ.

This journey to know God and make God known

did not happen in a day. It was a long process of seeking God that continues even today.

Instead of going to a traditional Bible college, God led me to a discipleship program called Master's Commission. The Master's Commission (MC) program began in Phoenix, AZ, under Tommy Barnett's ministry. It soon grew so that many churches all over the United States and even the world had their own MC programs.

The Master's Commission that I attended was at First Assembly of God in Lafayette, Indiana. Our MC averaged about 8–15 students while I was there. (Like any movement, methods change. MC is no longer in Lafayette. I'm thankful it was there when I needed it.) MC focused on accomplishing our Lord's Great Commission. It was a nine-month discipleship program that concentrated on knowing God and making God known.

Broken

When I first arrived at Master's Commission, I had a very legalistic attitude. My pride made me think that I was "perfect." Soon, God began purifying me so that I could see my own imperfections. He opened my eyes and began to break me.

When we seek the Lord, we are like silver that goes under the fire. All the impurities will rise to the surface.

My attitude was like the Pharisees or Sadducees. I looked down on others who were different or not as "holy" as me. I lacked compassion. The Lord broke me and taught me to love and give mercy and grace. When we are broken, God can remold us into his beautiful mosaic.

Ruth Stall, a missionary to Peru, once said, "If my life is broken when given to Jesus it is because pieces will feed a multitude, but a loaf will satisfy only a little lad."

When we are weak or broken, this is when we are made strong in Christ.

> *"My grace is sufficient for you, for my power is made perfect in weakness." Therefore I will boast all the more gladly about my weaknesses, so that Christ's power may rest on me. That is why, for Christ's sake, I delight in weaknesses, in insults, in hardships, in persecutions, in difficulties. For when I am weak, then I am strong (2 Corinthians 12:9–10).*

God's grace is more than enough. It's not about my abilities. It's about God's power working in me.

The Fear Factor

My MC directors, Todd and Candy Sitcler, were precisely the leaders I needed for that season of my life. They taught me to dream beyond myself. Pastor Todd would often say, "Dream so big that you will fail so that, when you succeed, you will know it was God."

Fear had stopped me from dreaming big. I didn't feel qualified, capable, or worthy of God-sized dreams. Yes, God had "called" me, but what would that look like? What could I possibly do for God? My fear of the unknown and fear of failure was stopping me from moving forward.

One of my biggest fears was public speaking. For years, I thought my shyness was just my personality. I honestly thought it was the way God had created me. Slowly, I realized that my shyness was actually fear. I was afraid of what people would think or say if I spoke my opinions or shared my faith. The Devil was trying to silence me. He didn't want me to share my faith and see souls saved.

The Lord has not given us a spirit of fear but of power, love, and a sound mind (2 Timothy 1:7, NKJV). Many of our churches have been silenced by the fear of the Enemy. It is time for the church to no longer be silent. We are called to walk in faith, not in fear.

Overcoming this fear was not a one-day miracle. I had to be intentional in getting outside of my comfort zone. The MC program provided many opportunities for me to push beyond my limits.

One beyond-me occasion involved speaking in front of a crowd. MC would often travel to minister at churches or youth ministries. During my first few months, they would just ask me to share my name, where I was from, and a Bible verse. That was enough to set my heart pounding and make me want to throw up. I remember freezing on stage once, and someone had to whisper the words into my ear.

Over time, I grew in my God-confidence. Then MC gave me the opportunity to share a three-minute testimony. Once this mountain was conquered, I shared just one point of a sermon. Finally, after a few years, I could share an entire sermon. Practice does make perfect!

Today I speak to hundreds and thousands of people on a regular basis. There is still a sense of nervousness before speaking that keeps me humble and dependent on the Holy Spirit. However, I no longer panic, because I know that God will give me the words to say.

On my journey to boldness, I memorized several verses that I still pray before speaking engagements:

I came to you in weakness with great fear and trembling. My message and my preaching were not with wise and persuasive words, but with a demonstration of the Spirit's power, so that your faith might not rest on human wisdom, but on God's power (1 Corinthians 2:3–5).

> *Pray also for me, that whenever I speak, words may be given me so that I will fearlessly make known the mystery of the gospel, for which I am an ambassador in chains. Pray that I may declare it fearlessly, as I should (Ephesians 6:19–20).*

My prayer is always that I would proclaim the message of Jesus fearlessly and simply so others can understand. The Holy Spirit must be the one who speaks through me so that those who hear will put their faith in God's power—not in human wisdom.

As I developed my voice, the other students gave me the nickname of "Sassy Sarah." I had to learn that not every word that comes to our minds should be spoken! God calls us to tame our tongues. We must say our words in love with great patience and understanding.

Another beyond-me occasion involved witnessing to non-believers. It's one thing to share your faith with someone who believes the same as you. It's an entirely different challenge to share it with someone who does not believe.

MC often sent us out to witness door-to-door or evangelize at the local university campus. When I was in the early stages of witnessing, Pastor Todd assigned me a partner: a fellow student named Sunshine. Yes, her name really was Sunshine, and her personality matched her name. I don't think Sunshine ever knew a stranger—everyone was her friend.

Jesus set the example by sending the disciples out to evangelize two-by-two. This method allowed me to observe how another Christian interacted with people. Sunshine would often introduce me, which then gave me a platform to speak. The more I witnessed to others, the easier it got.

Today, my heart pounds less from fear and more from a burden to reach the lost. Still, intentional evangelism remains outside of my comfort zone. There are some days when I don't want to leave my comfortable home, but I'm always glad when I do. Many times I've had at least one divine appointment by the end of the day.

When witnessing, we don't always see the fruit of the harvest right away. Sometimes we are only planting a seed. But the reality is that the crop is ready. It's amazing that when we are obedient to God and "go," He leads us to those who are willing to receive Him. Many people are crying out for answers to life and looking for hope.

When you do get to lead someone to the Lord, the joy is simply incredible. It makes evangelism almost addictive. Something that I used to hate and run away from has now become one of my dreams. This is what happens when we dream beyond ourselves.

Discover Your Hidden God-Given Gifts

I have always had a natural talent for art. From the time I was in elementary school, I consistently excelled in art classes. My high school art teacher even created an Advanced Painting 2 class so that I could keep painting. In my junior year of high school, my artwork was chosen for the cover of the yearbook! I remember feeling like I wanted to hide when I saw my painting in the hands of hundreds of students as they passed their books around to sign.

Today I still enjoy painting as a hobby. I've even used this talent for ministry. I've painted many youth logos on the walls of churches and also help with children's ministry by painting backdrops and sermon illustrations. Never underestimate how God can use your talents for His glory!

But have you ever had to do something that was beyond what you thought you were capable of?

In Master's Commission, we were forced to try every kind of ministry as part of discipleship. This required me to do things I'd never dreamed of. In fact, I hated some of the ministries. Maybe "hate" is a strong word; let's just say "greatly disliked." It was hard and uncomfortable. The crazy truth is that some of the activities I despised have become the ones I love the most.

God has given all of us talents and abilities. Even non-believers are talented. But God also wants to develop spiritual gifts inside of us. He desires to move us beyond our natural abilities into the supernatural. I believe some of our gifts are lying dormant. We need only to get out of the "box" of what we have always known and try new things. We also need to seek the Lord and ask to be empowered with spiritual gifts.

Some of my favorite people in Lafayette, Indiana, are Gary and Gayle Quinn. Gary owns a roofing company, and Gayle is now a retired schoolteacher. Neither Gary nor Gayle are official pastors—however, their ministry is one of the most fruitful and rewarding I have ever seen in my lifetime.

Gary used to take us to Purdue University with Scripture verses stapled to bags of potato chips. We would walk throughout the campus telling students that Jesus loved them. Honestly, I thought Gary was a little crazy, but I also admired his desire to reach lost souls.

Gary and Gayle ran the bus ministry at First Assembly of God. Every week they led JC (Jesus Christ) Club. Their Bible lessons were always engaging, and every kid knew they were loved.

One summer Gary even paid me, a poor student, to help him do sidewalk Sunday School in the welfare housing of Lafayette. Each day of the week we went to a different housing project and met kids under the shade of a tree. We had games, snacks, Bible stories, and the love of Jesus to share with them. (By the way, I used that money to go on my first overseas mission trip to Romania.)

Gary and Gayle reached the unloved and forgotten people of Lafayette. They sacrificed their time, money, and resources for Kingdom causes. If there was ever a couple who dreamed beyond themselves, I have to say, they get my vote.

The time I spent with Gary and Gayle taught me a lot about serving and loving others. They were "normal" people who used every talent and resource they had to further the message of Jesus. They did not waste their time on this earth but used it to disciple people like me and touch the forgotten communities around the church.

This couple looked beyond the four walls of the church into their community. They saw a need and found a way to meet it.

On August 2, 2005, I wrote in my journal:

> *God has laid on my heart that the church needs to realize that it's not a building. The church is people. It's not what people do inside the building that saves souls. It's what they do outside—in the world. We need to stop locking the message of Jesus inside a church building and start sharing Him with the lost. The church on the street will save souls.*

God's dream for each of us includes what we do outside of "church," not just inside the building. How can you use your talents as an accountant, nurse, or school teacher to make God's dream come true?

> God's dream for each of us includes what we do outside of "church," not just inside the building.

God places each of us in areas of influence. You meet people who I will never encounter. Your co-workers may never enter a church building, but they work alongside you eight hours a day, five days a week.

Have you discovered your talents? What are they? Could God be calling you to do something outside of your comfort zone that might reveal a hidden talent?

Faithful in the Small Things

Since our MC program was fairly small, I was asked to do tasks that probably would have been given to someone more qualified than me if there had been anyone else available.

God taught me to work with all my heart as if serving God, not man. "Whatever you do, work at it with all your heart, as working for the Lord, not for human masters, since you know that you will receive an inheritance from the Lord as a reward. It is the Lord Christ you are serving" (Colossians 3:23–24).

At first, my directors only gave me a few small tasks. As I proved my faithfulness and excellence in those small tasks, more and more were entrusted to me. "Whoever can be trusted with very little can also be trusted with much, and whoever is dishonest with very little will also be dishonest with much" (Luke 16:10).

Each task is a step toward accomplishing a goal or dream. Can others trust you with their dreams? If you take care of other people's dreams, then God will take care of yours.

Make Other People's Dreams Come True.

I was learning to dream big for my life. However, I recognized that God would only trust me with His dreams for me if I helped make other people's dreams come true.

God taught me to be an "armor bearer." When you're an armor bearer, you go into battle and fight alongside someone else. You fight for them and allow them to take credit for the victory. You protect their life and prepare the way for them.

Some of us are not called to be the "grand leader." We are called to be armor bearers. We may not be called to be the pastor but to be the volunteer leader or part of the support staff instead. Each of us has a different calling in the body of Christ. We can't all be the same, or the body wouldn't function properly.

"There are different kinds of gifts, but the same Spirit distributes them. There are different kinds of service, but the same Lord. There are different kinds of working, but in all of them and in everyone it is the same God at work" (1 Corinthians 12:4–6).

In the church world, we need to be careful not to become "spiritually envious." We should recognize our spiritual gifts and rejoice in them. There is no reason to compare ourselves to someone else.

The best way to kill your envy of someone is to help that person accomplish their dreams. Instead of criticizing them, support them. Help them prosper in their God-given ministry.

"Let us not become weary in doing good, for at the proper time we will reap a harvest if we do not give up" (Galatians 6:9).

The harvest doesn't mean praise or money. The Bible uses the word "harvest" to refer to lost souls finding Jesus Christ. Dreaming beyond yourself means helping make others' dreams come true so that God's dream can come true.

Bloom Where You Are Planted.

Sometimes our dreams are for the ends of the earth. We long to go somewhere else—anywhere else. I've learned that we need to bloom where God has planted us.

If I have a dream of witnessing to thousands in Africa, but I can't even be faithful to witness in America, why would God entrust me with another continent? The same applies to Africans and others throughout the world. Start where God has placed you. Then He will trust you with more.

Just as Joseph "bloomed" in Potiphar's house and the prison, we also need to make the best of our situations. Don't crawl into a corner and have a pity party about how bad your life is. Find the best in every day the Lord has made!

God wants to use where you are to prepare you for where you will be.

God wants to use where you are to prepare you for where you will be.

If you are in school, you must pass an exam before you move to the next grade level. The same is true in life. Don't rush through what God is trying to teach you. Listen to your heavenly professor. Learn and make use of every teachable moment.

The dream is bigger than you. God needs you to rely on Him and listen to His voice. He is orchestrating things behind the scenes that you can't see yet.

Wherever God has planted you, don't move until you know that you have heard His voice. If a plant is uprooted over and over again, it loses its strength and dies.

God wants you to put down deep roots and hold onto your integrity so that the storms of life won't blow you away.

Cursed is the one who trusts in man, who draws strength from mere flesh and whose heart turns away from the Lord. . . . But blessed is the one who trusts in the Lord, whose confidence is in him. They will be like a tree planted by the water that sends out its roots by the stream. It does not fear when heat comes; its leaves are always green. It has no worries in a year of drought and never fails to bear fruit (Jeremiah 17:5, 7–8).

Is there fruit in your life? Have your roots grown deep into streams of Living Water? Or are you trusting in your own strength and abilities?

A few years ago, I wrote these words to encourage a friend. I pray they would now encourage you:

God wants you to know that you are not a failure in "ministry." It is not an accident you [served in the ministries of the church]. God led you there, and you made yourself available. Your heart to serve was God's heart. Jesus came not to be served but to serve.

To be a "minister" of the gospel does not mean you have to be a great preacher or have a Bible degree. God uses [all people] in His Kingdom. The only thing God desires is someone who says, "Lord, I will deny myself, take up my cross and follow you" (Luke 9:23). God wants available people who will trust in Him.

God created you with skills and talents. He made you, [insert your name here]. He didn't make you like me or anyone else. He made you different because you can use those skills for His Kingdom in ways we never can. He wants you to stop comparing yourself and feeling like you are not good enough. He created you—therefore you are more than good enough. He loves that you think outside of the box because He created you that way.

At the same time—He is calling you, like Peter, to step out of the boat. Stop relying on your "natural" abilities and trust in Jesus that you can walk on water. The Holy Spirit empowers us to do what we cannot do ourselves.

God is calling you to walk by faith, not by sight. Remember, He chooses the weak and foolish people so that God gets the glory and we cannot boast that it was our natural ability—it was God!

You will never feel ready. The world says "ready, set, go,"[1] but in God's Kingdom, you have to take a step of faith and just go. Eventually, you will realize that God enabled you to be ready.[2]

The Lord never gives us the big picture because honestly, we would probably be so afraid we would never go. Instead, He gives us just enough light in the darkness of the unknown to take the next step He has for us. We cannot worry about tomorrow but should trust God in every moment of every day. If we trust God—we know that nothing is wasted and God works all things for our good.

I pray that these words will encourage you. I don't know your tomorrows—only God does. Thankfully, God does know! So trust in Him. Rely on and seek the Holy Spirit's empowerment. God is calling you beyond the natural to the supernatural.

Don't allow the Devil to discourage you and stop you from winning the battle. Joshua 1:9 says, "Have I not commanded you? Be strong and courageous. Do not be afraid; do not be discouraged, for the Lord your God will be with you wherever you go."

Will you dream beyond your natural abilities? God is calling you to rely on His power and His strength to accomplish His dream.

CHAPTER THREE:
JUST AROUND THE CORNER (GOD'S CONFIRMATION)

"Then I heard the voice of the Lord saying, 'Whom shall I send? And who will go for us?' And I said, 'Here am I, Send me!'"
—Isaiah 6:8

When God calls, He confirms.

We must patiently wait for God's timing to open the right doors and close the wrong ones. But how will we know when something is God's will for our lives? And when God confirms, will we obey?

When I was a child, missions was my passion. Some days I was sure that God wanted me to be a missionary. On other days, I felt unqualified. Maybe God only wanted me to pray for and support missionaries?

Then I began to dream beyond myself. What if God *could* use me?

During my second year at Master's Commission, I was required to complete a ministry project about what I wanted to do with my life. Funny enough, I did my project on being a pastor's wife. (This dream has still not become a reality. The pastor never came, so I became the pastor.) Part of our assignment was to interview three people. I chose to speak to the local pastor's wife and two missionary wives.

One of the missionary wives was Teresa Trout. I remember Teresa challenging me to come to Africa. How could I know I was called if I never went? It was impressed on my heart to go to Africa for six months. I took steps to apply as a missionary associate with the Assemblies of

How could I know I was called if I never went?

God World Missions. I dreamed of serving in Africa with the Trout family, my childhood pastors. However, this door soon closed as the Trouts felt God leading them to return to the USA and pastor their home church in Greencastle, Indiana.

The other missionary wife I interviewed was Delight Peercy. Delight and her husband, Wayne, were missionaries in South Africa, and they were living in Lafayette temporarily while they raised funds and worked through some transitions. Wayne and Delight adopted me into their family. On Easter Sunday, I had to help with ministry at the church, so the Peercy family invited me to spend the holiday with them. On many occasions, I was welcomed into their home to sip hot chocolate and talk about life.

Wayne and Delight Peercy were another God-appointed couple in my life journey. I loved that they loved Africa. They had four sons around my age and also two adopted daughters who were born in South Africa. I asked them about possibly serving with them on the mission field. They loved me and supported the idea, but because they were transitioning from one assignment to another, the mission office was unable to place me with them.

Maybe I was limiting God by trying to go only with people I knew? I decided to open my application to go anywhere in Africa. However, doors kept closing. The office even asked me, "Have you considered Europe?" Africa was where I knew God wanted me, so I decided to wait on the Lord to open the right door in His time. In the meantime, I would continue to serve in ministry and prepare myself for the calling.

Three years passed from the time I applied to when God opened the door. While I was waiting, I felt God encourage me to keep doing the last thing He had told me to do. I continued to volunteer with Master's Commission, learning leadership roles, discipleship, youth ministry, and many other skills.

I also completed my correspondence courses to become an ordained minister with the Assemblies of God through Berean School of the Bible with Global University in Springfield, Missouri. They sent me the graduation information, but I threw it all away, assuming they would mail me my diploma. Paying to travel to Springfield for a graduation ceremony with people I had never met did not seem realistic.

Then I received an email from Global University. "You have been chosen as the Student Reflection Speaker for Berean School of the Bible at the graduation ceremony!" I actually replied to this email to ask if they were "legit." How could I, of all the possible people, have been chosen? They assured me that I was indeed the chosen speaker and all my expenses would be paid to come to the ceremony with a friend or relative.

My sister and I drove eight hours to Missouri for me to give the student reflection speech. At this time in my life, I was still very new to public speaking, so I was quite intimidated. The other speakers were from Finland and Ghana. I was "Sarah Careins from Indiana." Indiana didn't sound very impressive.

After I had made it through my speech, I was welcomed to enjoy a reception. Here I spoke with some former missionaries to the Philippians. I shared with them how I was trying to get to Africa, but God had closed the door. Upon hearing this, their eyes lit up, and they said, "The area director of South Africa is sitting right over there. Come, we'll introduce you."

A month later, the area director personally called me to say I was approved to go to South Africa with Wayne and Delight Peercy. I raised my funds within the next month, which was a huge miracle. When God wants to open the door, He opens it wide!

How Can I Confirm If This Is God's Dream for Me?

We all want to know God's dream for our lives. His ultimate goal is for us to save souls, but this can happen in a variety of ways. God doesn't call everyone to be a missionary. He also calls doctors, teachers, accountants, farmers, and so on. He uses *all* people in *all* places.

Should I take this job? Should I move to a new city? Is this the person I should marry?

How can I confirm I'm doing what God wants?

The truth is that God will reveal His will to us when the time is right. We must trust in Him and prepare ourselves to hear and understand God's dream when He does speak.

Even Jesus prayed "not my will, but yours be done" (Luke 22:42). Knowing and doing God's will is not always easy.

Here are seven principles to help you confirm God's specific dream for your life.[3]

1. You must believe in Jesus Christ as your Lord and Savior.

*"For those who are led by the Spirit of God
are the children of God."*
—Romans 8:14

If you are not a child of God, then you cannot expect to hear from God. Only those who are in right relationship with God will be able to know His dream for their lives. Those who are not children of God are like people driving in the dark without a light or wandering in the fog not knowing if they are going in the right direction. The light of truth can only shine and make your path clear when you have put your faith in Jesus Christ.

Being born again is the first step to finding God's will. If you are backslidden or have never surrendered your life to Christ, ask Him to come into your heart today and forgive your sins.

2. You must pray.

*"Do not be anxious about anything, but in
every situation, by prayer and petition,
with thanksgiving, present your requests to God."*
—Philippians 4:6

"If any of you lacks wisdom, he should ask God,
who gives generously to all without finding fault,
and it will be given to him."
—James 1:5

Prayer should never be the last resort. It should be a regular part of our daily lives. Talk to God about everything in your heart, including your need for guidance and understanding of His will.

When you pray, don't expect God to show you the next 10 to 20 years of your life. God only promises to supply our daily bread. Take one day at a time.

Be willing to accept God's answer to your prayers. Sometimes He says "yes" and other times "no." Then sometimes, it's "not yet." Remember, His dream for you is always the best, and He knows when the time is right.

3. You must live a godly life.

"Do not conform to the pattern of this world,
but be transformed by the renewing of your mind.
Then you will be able to test and approve what
God's will is—his good, pleasing and perfect will."
—Romans 12:2

"If you love me, keep my commands."
—John 14:15

The key to knowing God's will is godliness (living in a way that pleases God).

Because we love God, we need to act upon the principles God teaches us and obey what He commands. We are on a journey of being transformed into the likeness of Christ. Of course, we all make mistakes. We will only reach one hundred percent perfection when we get to Heaven, but we should continually seek to please God. Without holiness, no one will see the Lord (Hebrews 12:14b).

When we accept God's dream for our lives, we turn away from our selfish sins and toward God. Being in God's will is worth any sacrifice or challenge that comes with living a godly life.

4. You must study the Scriptures.

"Your word is a lamp for my feet, a light on my path."
—Psalm 119:105

God's dream for mankind is the theme of the entire Bible. If you desire to know His will for you, study the Scriptures. God has already given us many principles to live by to fulfill His plans. We must do our part: reading, studying, and obeying.

For example, one principle is to "seek first his kingdom and his righteousness" (Matthew 6:33). What are you putting first in your life? Your job, friends, money, or something else? God isn't against you experiencing joy in these areas, but He does want to be first. He wants to be your ultimate dream.

5. You must listen to the Holy Spirit.

"But when he, the Spirit of truth, comes, he will guide you into all truth."
—John 16:13a

Too many people go around claiming "God told me . . ." when in fact, God said nothing to them at all. Occasionally, God will speak in an audible voice, but this is not His usual method.

The Holy Spirit's guidance often comes as a steady impression. We think about it day and night. It doesn't leave us. These impressions should always be confirmed with Scripture; they should never contradict each other.

The Holy Spirit's communication will guide us to a place where He can use us. For example, in Acts 8, Philip is led by the Spirit to witness about Christ to the Ethiopian eunuch. As a result, the man is saved and baptized.

The Holy Spirit's communication will guide us to a place where He can use us.

The Holy Spirit also gives us peace and confirms when we are on track and doing God's will. If we get off track, the Spirit will be quick to show us that too.

God may also speak through dreams, visions, and even angels. I do not mean that every dream we have at night means something. However, we must be ready to listen to the Holy Spirit and discern when God is speaking.

6. You must understand that God uses circumstances to direct the lives of His people.

"But I will stay on at Ephesus until Pentecost, because a great door for effective work has opened to me, and there are many who oppose me."
—1 Corinthians 16:8–9

In Acts 19, Paul arrived in Ephesus and faced tremendous opposition. Why would he decide to stay and not leave? Paul did not necessarily hear a voice from Heaven saying, "Remain in Ephesus." He saw the way God was moving and saving souls in the city and the need to disciple new converts, and he knew that it was not yet time for him to leave.

Think of circumstances as God's traffic lights. What are the lights for? If you are driving, they will tell you when to go and when to stop. Many accidents occur when people do not pay attention to the traffic signs. In the Christian life, God often uses circumstances to guide us.

It is foolish to go ahead and do something when God has already tried to show you not to do it. Proverbs 22:3 says, "The prudent see danger and take refuge, but the simple keep going and pay the penalty."

But you may ask, can't Satan hinder us or destroy our faith by placing obstacles in our path? How can I know if it's the Devil, God, or myself?

Remember that Satan is not all-knowing like God. He and his demons have their limitations. They cannot know God's will and the Spirit's leading for every child of God.

"For who knows a person's thoughts except their own spirit within them? In the same way no one knows the thoughts of God except the Spirit of God" (1 Corinthians 2:11).

God is not the author of confusion. Ask God to bring clarity. All the Enemy can do is harass us, attempt to confuse us as we seek God's will, and try to hinder us with obstacles after God has given clear direction.

In Matthew 21:21, Jesus says, "Truly I tell you, if you have faith and do not doubt, not only can you do what was done to the fig tree, but also you can say to this mountain, 'Go, throw yourself into the sea,' and it will be done." Jesus wanted us to know that we have the authority to tear down anything the Devil would put in our way.

7. You must understand that God uses other people to direct His people.

"The way of fools seems right to them, but the wise listen to advice."
—Proverbs 12:15

"Surely you need guidance to wage war, and victory is won through many advisers."
—Proverbs 24:6

How do you feel about asking for advice? It is not a sign of weakness; the Bible says it is a wise thing to do.

No matter how smart you think you are, you should seek the counsel of godly people. By talking it over, you allow God to intervene and speak into your life.

The key is talking to the *right* people—those who love God and are full of the Spirit. A wise counselor is often known for their wisdom. They should demonstrate the fruit of godliness, serve the Lord faithfully, and always want God's best for your life. If you ask a foolish person, you will probably get a foolish answer.

Unfamiliar Paths

The most fulfilled people are those who know God's will and do it.

In January 2007, I stepped off a plane into South Africa for the first time. We drove in the dark for over three hours to reach the Peercy home in Polokwane, the main city of the Limpopo Province. As soon as we arrived, I fell asleep. When I woke up the next morning, I heard noises outside and thought it might be monkeys. I peered out the window and realized that it was only the sound of birds. This would not be the first time my assumptions were proven wrong. Africa had a lot to teach me.

Africa was challenging, but it was a dream come true for me. The next six months would be filled with powerful ministry and seeking God's dream for my life.

Did God want me to give my life as a missionary to Africa?

The Scripture verse that God impressed on my heart for this African journey was Isaiah 42:16. "I will lead the blind by ways they have not known, along unfamiliar paths I will guide them; I will turn the darkness into light before them and make rough places smooth. These are the things I will do; I will not forsake them."

God will guide us through unfamiliar paths and into the light. He will not forsake us.

As a youth, I loved to read books (I hope you are enjoying this one). One of my favorite stories was about Jim Elliot and Nate Saint, men who ministered to the Huaorani Tribe in Ecuador. Before dying as a martyr, Jim Elliot wrote in his journal, "He is no fool who gives what he cannot keep to gain what he cannot lose." This quotation led me to realize that being a missionary would require great sacrifice.

My battle in becoming a missionary was over the fact that I would have to give up my family. This was my biggest struggle. It still is.

One of the promises God gave me was Matthew 19:29: "And everyone who has left houses or brothers or sisters or father or mother or wife or children or fields for my sake will receive a hundred times as much and will inherit eternal life."

Could I trust God to take care of my family?

Romans 12:1 says, "Therefore, I urge you, brothers and sisters, in view of God's mercy, to offer your bodies as a living sacrifice, holy and pleasing to God—this is your true and proper worship."

Many people give to missions. The offering plate passes by, and you put in a few bucks. Few people put their lives in the offering plate. They choose to become the offering and be the living sacrifice. This is true worship.

On March 6, 2007, I received an email from a family friend who declared that I was called to be a missionary long-term. She said, "It's obvious." However, it wasn't yet obvious to me.

Lord, I will do whatever You want. I will be available to do Your will. Please give me the strength to do it. It's such a sacrifice to leave my family and friends. I think it would be very difficult to be single and on the mission field. . . . I do know it would be worth it. To make such a huge decision, I need a huge confirmation. I need to know it's God. I have faith that the Lord will indeed let me know. I'm thankful for what the Lord has given me now. I thank You, Lord, for the lives I'm impacting through You.

Not only am I impacting lives here in Africa, but my emails are challenging to those back in the States. Thank You, Lord, for choosing me. I pray that I would prove faithful and worthy of Your trust. I humbly come before You knowing that I am nothing without You. I ask for Your Holy Spirit to fill me and go before me. I love You, Lord.

Just like Gideon in Judges 6:17, I said, "If now I have found favor in your eyes, give me a sign that it is really you talking to me." By the end of that month, I had received my "sign" from the Lord.

On March 28, 2007, at 8:00 a.m. I wrote this:

I believe I've received a bit of a revelation.

The Lord had me remember working with Adopt-a-Block. Every Saturday we would knock on the same doors of a neighborhood block asking if we could do their yard work for free. Of course we had a few people that would allow us to help them and we built good relationships with them. However, the majority of the houses didn't want help—but we would continue to knock on their door and still ask them every week.

I realized when I took over this ministry that we were wasting our time. What if just around the corner and two houses down there was a lady who was willing to receive Christ? But we never got to her because we spent our time with those who were rejecting us.

So we changed Adopt-a-Block. We would knock on everyone's door only once a season. We then spent our time with those who were accepting the help. This way, we ministered to many more people by reaching more houses.

God spoke to me that, in the same way, America is like those houses that you continually knock on with continual rejection. Of course, there are a few who desire help. However, just around the corner is Africa who is crying out for help. Their door is open wide, desiring us to come in. God is saying to go where the harvest is plentiful and ready—and where the laborers are few. . . .

. . . I will go and labor.

Just around the corner from America is Africa. The needs are so great. In America, you will often have one church with many pastors. In Africa, you have one pastor with many churches. People are ready to receive Christ. All they need is someone who will go "knock on their door" and share the message of God's love with them.

How, then, can they call on the one they have not believed in? And how can they believe in the one of whom they have not heard? And how can they hear without someone preaching to them? And how can anyone preach unless they are sent? As it is written, "How beautiful are the feet of those who bring good news!" (Romans 10:14–15).

What is God telling you? What is "just around your corner" that you have neglected? Is God's dream for you just around the corner of your cubicle at the office? Is it the student sitting at the desk next to you?

What Will I Do When I Get There?

Sometimes God uses an idea to get us moving in one direction when in reality He will take us in another. Now that I felt called to full-time missions, I wondered what I could do. The first thought was that I could help start a Master's Commission in South Africa. This is what I knew and was comfortable with, but it was not what I ended up doing.

I was asked to help with youth ministry. In fact, I was invited to help relaunch the National Youth Ministries for the International Assemblies of God in South Africa. Just to remind you—I'd never even been a youth pastor before! I'd only assisted a youth pastor.

I felt unqualified . . . but called to step out in faith.

In Acts 16:6–15, Paul starts his second missionary journey. Paul also had a plan, but God redirected him to Macedonia, "just around the corner."

*Paul and his companions traveled throughout the region of Phrygia and Galatia, having been kept by the Holy Spirit from preaching the word in the province of Asia. When they came to the border of Mysia, they tried to enter Bithynia, but the **Spirit of Jesus would not allow them to**. So they passed by Mysia and went down to Troas. During the night **Paul had a vision of a man of Macedonia standing and begging him, "Come over to Macedonia and help us."** After Paul had seen the vision, we got ready at once to leave for Macedonia, concluding that God had called us to preach the gospel to them.*

From Troas we put out to sea and sailed straight for Samothrace, and the next day we went on to Neapolis. From there we traveled to Philippi, a Roman colony and the leading city of that district of Macedonia. And we stayed there several days.

*On the Sabbath we went outside the city gate to the river, where we **expected to find a place of prayer**. We sat down and **began to speak to the women who had gathered there.** One of those listening was a woman from the city of Thyatira named Lydia, a dealer in purple cloth. She was a worshiper of God. **The Lord opened her heart to respond to Paul's message.** When she and the members of her household were baptized, she invited us to her home. "If you consider me a believer in the Lord," she said, **"come and stay at my house."** And she persuaded us [emphasis added].*

The Holy Spirit guided Paul to change direction and go to Macedonia. Once he received confirmation, he did not delay. They "got ready at once to leave for Macedonia." Paul did not have all the details, but He trusted in the vision/dream God had given him.

Here are a few lessons we can learn from Paul's missionary journey to Macedonia.

1. God does not always guide us in the way we expect.

Paul planned to go to Bithynia, but God prevented him from going there. He led Paul through a vision to go to Macedonia—a place he had never been. God not only guides us to the right places but he also guides us away from the wrong places. Paul wanted to preach the gospel in Bithynia. How could that be wrong? "Wrong" could be "right," but it may not be God's plan for this time. Trust the guidance of the Holy Spirit.

As you seek God's dream, be prepared for the unexpected. Don't worry. God will guide you and take you further than you've ever been.

2. Don't feel like you have to organize a great work for God—rather, let God start the work in a small way.

When Paul went to Macedonia, he simply went to find a place to pray. As he was doing that, God brought Lydia across his path. They simply shared the gospel with her, and that resulted in her and her household being saved. Prayer is always the best way to start a lasting work. God will bring the people and open the doors for His work.

3. God will meet your physical needs.

God provided housing for Paul through Lydia. Wherever God calls us, He will provide for us. Sometimes this is our biggest step of faith. Rest assured, God will meet your needs.

4. God will bring co-workers to labor with you.

Previously in Acts, we read how God provided Silas and Timothy. Then in 16:11, the "we" shows that the author Luke has also joined the journey. God will send you a Silas, Timothy, and Luke to be co-workers with you. You will also meet Lydias who will eventually become co-laborers with the gospel.

5. God will give you joy when life gets tough.

In Acts 16:16–40, Paul and Silas are beaten and thrown into prison. Instead of being angry and upset, they pray and sing hymns to God. Suddenly, there is an earthquake. God changes their circumstances through their praise!

Paul and Silas chose not to run away from a difficult situation. They were more interested in leading the jailer and his family to salvation than gaining their freedom! Remember to keep a positive attitude in difficulties— what may seem like a terrible circumstance might bring more people to salvation through Jesus Christ.

Sometimes, there is a place to witness just around the corner from where we have been looking. Has God closed one door only to open another? Where is your Macedonia? God will confirm His dream for you if you listen and wait on Him. When He does confirm, be ready to go.

This was my prayer on January 26, 2007 (my second day in Africa). May it also be yours now:

> *Lord, I'm really going to need your help. I want to make an impact on this world. Please guide and direct my path. Show me what to do. Give me discernment. I ask that you would give me your words to speak. Help me to show your love like no one could fathom. Give me boldness to love others. Speak to my heart and show me what to preach. Break evil spirits, heal the hurting, set the captives free. Fill me with your Holy Spirit. Anoint me for your work. Enable me. Open doors. Provide divine appointments. Touch the people of [South Africa **or insert your place here**] and let them feel your love, peace, and joy. I feel unqualified. Please empower me with your Spirit.*

PART TWO

TRUST THE DREAM-GIVER

CHAPTER FOUR:
BEGGARS
(GOD, MY PROVIDER)

*And my God will meet all your needs according to the
riches of his glory in Christ Jesus.*
—Philippians 4:19

Your dreams will stretch your faith. When the dream
is bigger than you, you have to trust the Dream-Giver
to provide for it. If God has called you somewhere, He
will provide the means to get you there.

When I was a child, my parents gave me $2.50 as an
allowance each week for doing chores around the house.
They taught me to tithe 25 cents every week (Malachi
3:10). Since my parents always gave me everything I
needed, why would I need the $2.25 left over? So I
also gave $2.00 to missions every month (Philippians
4:15–16).

God calls us to be givers, not just receivers. The tithe is giving 10 percent of all your income back to God. This is not optional. It's obedience. In fact, God owns it all! We are just stewards of the resources He has given us. One day I'd love to live on the 10 percent and give God back the 90 percent.

My parents lived from paycheck to paycheck. There wasn't a lot of "extra" money. But my parents set an example of tithing and giving. They also sacrificed to give to missions. By the world's standards, my parents were rich. By America's standards, we were poor enough to receive government lunches at school. My parents were too proud to accept help, so we packed our lunches. Once each week, we were allowed to buy a school lunch at the cafeteria. Packing my lunch wasn't the "cool" thing to do, but I was fed, and my meal was packed with love. Sometimes my mom would even put little notes inside the lunchbox that said, "I love you. Hope you have a great day at school."

As a youth in the Assemblies of God churches, I helped raise money for missionary vehicles on the mission field. I sold candy bars, collected old soda cans to turn in for change, washed cars, baked for dessert sales, participated in walk-a-thons, and took part in so many other fundraisers. I also sacrificed the money I earned by doing small jobs.

As a new missionary in South Africa, I received one of those vehicles. In all of those years I gave, I didn't know that I would also receive.

Money for Missions

God usually grows my faith in small steps.

The first big step of faith was to raise money for my first home mission trip to New Orleans, Louisiana, where we would witness on the street to people attending the Mardi Gras celebration.

"Mardi Gras" is French for Fat Tuesday. Traditionally, it was the last night of eating fatty foods before Ash Wednesday, which marks the beginning of Lent (a 40-day fast leading up to Easter). On Ash Wednesday, some churches have priests put ashes in the shape of a cross on congregants' foreheads as a reminder of repentance.

This is one tradition that may have started off well, but modern culture has blown it out of proportion. Now the goal of Mardi Gras seems to be "sin as much as you can." Mardi Gras includes a lot of alcohol consumption and a ritual of guys handing out beads for girls to lift their shirts and show their breasts. If a girl has a lot of beads around her neck, it means a lot of guys have seen her exposed. This traditional celebration is now a place of darkness with many lost people who need to find true repentance and salvation.

The cost of going on this evangelism trip was $300. At the time, I didn't even have $30, so $300 seemed like an enormous amount of money. I sent out letters to my family and friends asking for their support. I bravely wrote that if more money came in, I would put it toward my Bible classes. Amazingly, one supporter wrote me a check for the full $300! The rest of the money given was enough for me to pay off my Bible courses for the semester.

When I arrived in the French Quarter, the center of the celebration, tarot card readers and witches had set up their tables for clients. My skin crawled as I felt the demonic presence. For the first time in my life, I *felt* evil. My witnessing partner and I decided we would go up to one of the tarot card readers to witness to her. She was dressed in an old Victorian gown and had painted a beard on her face. As we got closer, she began to whisper in a deep voice, "Go away . . . go away." Well, we went away. Sadly, my faith wasn't yet big enough to take on demonic powers.

The Mardi Gras trip taught me that God is my Provider! If He calls us, He will make a way. I also learned that often a mission trip teaches us more than we teach others. This first trip opened my eyes to the spiritual battle raging over lost souls.

The next trip I needed money for was a trip to Romania in October 2006. By this time, I was already planning to go to South Africa in January 2007, so I didn't feel right asking people for money for both. Instead, I worked all summer long and used my hard-earned money to travel for the first time to a foreign land.

Romania confirmed my call to Africa. While I was there, I met a taxi driver from Nigeria. Some of the missionaries had served in Swaziland, so I talked with them about Africa the entire time. Then, when we went to see the babies who had been abandoned in the hospital, God whispered to me, "At least these babies were left in the hospital. In Africa, they are thrown down pit toilets and left for dead on the side of the road." Romania was my sacrifice to help others, but in the end, God continued telling me to go to Africa.

Sent by God through Others

I planned to spend six months in Africa, but I needed about $10,000. Once again, I wrote to friends and family asking for their support.

I remember getting a phone call at midnight from another missionary. He had just received a $10,000 offering and said that God told him to tithe $1,000 of it to my mission trip. After I had spoken at the graduation ceremony, Global University gave me $1,000 for the mission trip. The rest of the money came in 10s, 20s, 50s, and 100s. Every donation got me one step closer to Africa. By the end of 2006, I had raised $12,000.

At the end of my first trip to Africa, a young student named Tumishang Sharlotte wrote me a poem:

Remember Me
I remember the days
when tears were striding down my face
when my heart was aching.
When there seemed to be
no way to escape the pain.
But then God chose you.
He chose you to come & rescue me.
I remember the day when
I regained my strength.
The day you prayed for me
In the middle of the school.
I felt the presence of God within me.
I felt I was floating.
Thank God he sent you here,
if you didn't I would still be hurting.
For He helped you chase away the evil spirit.
Halleluyah.

God sent me to South Africa. Everyone who gave to the trip also sent me. They were a part of the miracle in Tumishang's heart.

Am I Just a Beggar?

As soon as I returned home from South Africa in mid-2007, I began the process of becoming a fully appointed missionary with the Assemblies of God. This meant an entire year of raising funds. I had a one-time cash amount for expenses like plane tickets, and also a monthly budget of about $6,000. When you add up the money for all four years I would be in South Africa, it amounts to almost $300,000!

Now I would need to spend an entire year doing nothing but traveling to churches and raising funds for the work. I was just an average girl, so when I called churches, most people had no idea who I was. They didn't know if they could trust this young person to preach at their churches. It took a while for me to build my reputation. There were some discouraging days.

There was even a moment when I began to feel like the lame beggar sitting at the gate called Beautiful. I felt like I was begging for money to get to Africa. Some of my distant relatives even commented, "When are you going to get a real job?"

While I was attending a fundraising seminar, God rebuked that thought. He said, "You are not the lame beggar! You are Peter and John. You are the one bringing the miracle."

> *Then Peter said, "Silver or gold I do not have, but what I have I give you. In the name of Jesus Christ of Nazareth, walk." Taking him by the right hand, he helped him up, and instantly the man's feet and ankles became strong. He jumped to his feet and began to walk. Then he went with them into the temple courts, walking and jumping, and praising God (Acts 3:6–8).*

It is very humbling to ask other people for help. We want to work for it ourselves. We may not have any silver or gold, but we do have the power of God. The

Lord wants you to know that you are not the lame beggar. You are the one bringing the miracle! Dream beyond yourself and your situation. God will provide to accomplish His dreams.

> The Lord wants you to know that you are not the lame beggar. You are the one bringing the miracle!

At the same time, God says that we must ask before we receive. A beggar asks with persistence. We shouldn't be afraid to ask for God's provision. He promises that He will hear our requests.

As I was raising funds, I felt bad about getting money from people who had less than I did. I didn't want to accept their gifts because I felt they needed it more than me.

Then God reminded me of the story of the prophet Elijah and the widow of Zarephath (1 Kings 17:7–16). God commanded a widow to supply Elijah with food. She only had enough for one last meal with her son before they died from starvation. In obedience and faith, she gave her last meal to Elijah. God performed a miracle of provision with the jar of flour and oil. They did not run out until the rain came again.

We have to be willing to allow others to sacrifice for us. Their act of obedience may very well be for their own provision and blessing. By allowing others to participate in God's work through giving, we are allowing them to participate in the miracles and experience God's own provision.

God has challenged me to give more to missions than I ever have before. How can I expect others to give to me if I don't give to others? God gives us blessings so that we will be a blessing. I believe some of the most faithful supporters of missionaries are other missionaries.

Pimps and Beggars

In South Africa, there are beggars on almost every city street corner. These beggars may even have "pimps" who drop them off each morning at various locations. These pimps collect the beggars at the end of the day and claim most of their earnings. Giving financially to a beggar will only make the problem continue.

I don't want my heart to grow hard and lack compassion. I see the beggars' sad faces and torn clothes as they tap on my window asking for spare change or something to eat. It breaks my heart every time. When I see a young lady with her children on the street corner, I want to take them home and care for them . . . but I can't.

Rolling your window down to help a beggar or street vendor often results in a car hijacking. As a single lady, I've chosen to keep my windows rolled up. It's hard to not help those in need, but would my gift help the long-term problem? Wouldn't I be contributing to their "slavery" by the pimp?

I fear that I won't be the "good Samaritan" in Jesus' parable (Luke 10). I fear that when someone is truly hurting, I will just pass by on the other side of the road because I don't want to be inconvenienced. I really do want to bandage their wounds and care for their needs. I pray that God will give me discernment for who I should help.

Can I Be Trusted?

Another reason I struggle to give to beggars is that I don't know where the money will go. Will it just buy them drugs or alcohol? There have been times when I've bought someone food and then watched them sell it to someone else for cash. We are in a society that can no longer trust people to do what they say they will do.

This is why accountability is so important in missions. If someone gives to mission work, they want to know that they have made a wise investment. They want to trust that the money is going to the purpose for which they gave it.

Financial accountability is necessary to protect the giver and the worker. Receipts should be kept, and reports need to be made. There should be no appearance of evil. If someone were to audit me, there should be no mistakes or embezzled funds.

If money is given for a certain purpose, it must go to that designated cause. Don't think you will just "borrow" the money and pay it back later. If you didn't get permission to use the money, it's stealing.

When people can trust that their money is going to a worthy cause and they can see the outcome, they will keep giving. Most disciples want to give to the work of reaching lost people. It's just a matter of showing others that there is accountability and the money will indeed go where it was intended.

Are you giving to make God's dreams come true?

Today's Africa

Many people imagine Africans living in mud huts with lions roaming the streets. This is not the reality for most of Africa. Today's population is increasingly moving to the city centers for the universities, employment, and convenience. Africa is urbanizing faster than any other people group in the world.[4]

As I work with university students, I see that the young people of Africa are moving to the cities. If our churches do not find a way to reach them, we will lose them. My heart is to see urban properties purchased and renovated for inner-city churches in Africa. This will take millions of dollars. The dream is bigger than me, but possible with God.

God asks every believer to give (Heb. 13:16; 2 Corinthians 8:2; Acts 30:35). I believe Africa will be able to fund Africa's mission. America's money is not the answer to the world's needs. It doesn't mean that Americans should stop giving, but it is a call for others to give as well.

One African pastor recently wrote this to me after our trip to Mozambique for a university ministry conference:

> *The Holy Spirit is leading the African church to step out of being concerned about its internal poverty and to look to the outside world to see the real need. The testimony about France and Japan was a wake-up call to realize that while Africa is known as a receiver, it can be a giver. The church in Africa is rich in faith and the Word that can impact nations.*

One of the initiatives we have started with our youth ministry in South Africa is called Plant-to-Harvest. We have designed the first opportunity for the young people of our South African churches to give to mission work and to go on mission trips. Plant-to-Harvest is about planting a seed to reap a harvest of souls for the Kingdom of God. In the past few years, we have seen the youth begin to give. We also held our first mission trip. It has been exciting to see African young people catch a desire to do missions.

Missionaries are no longer just "white" people who come from the Western world. God is calling *all* people of *all* nations to *go* into *all* the world.

Is God calling you to missions?

What is stopping you? Is it the money?

Will you take a step of faith and believe for God to provide?

Are you supporting mission work?

If you aren't giving to others, then why should you receive?

My prayer is that we would create a culture of giving and going. The biggest gift you can give is your life!

Where Is Your Treasure?

"For where your treasure is, there your heart will be also."
—Matthew 6:21

Where is your treasure? You can tell a lot by the way someone spends their money. If you look at where your money goes every month, does it look like your treasure is God's work? Is it clothes? Is it airtime to call your friends?

The rich young ruler wanted to have eternal life. He had followed all the church "rules." But Jesus said, "One thing you lack. Go, sell everything you have and give to the poor, and you will have treasure in heaven. Then come, follow me" (Mark 10:21b). But this young man went away sad. He wasn't willing to give up his worldly wealth to follow Jesus.

In today's culture, it is easy to get caught up in the desire to attain worldly wealth. You can make this your "god." It can be what drives you every day. I've seen others focus on obtaining material possessions, yet many end up unfulfilled and in debt. They always want a bigger house or a better car. They are never satisfied.

Many Americans think of missionaries as poor people. However, most Africans think of American missionaries as rich. It's all about perspective. I believe that I am rich in God no matter how much money I have! He gives me food to eat and shelter.

> *So do not worry, saying, "What shall we eat?" or "What shall we drink?" or "What shall we wear?" For the pagans run after all these things, and your heavenly Father knows that you need them. But seek first his kingdom and his righteousness, and all these things will be given to you as well (Matthew 6:31–33).*

I need to seek God's dream first, and then He will take care of the provision. I don't need to worry. God is the creator of the earth. He owns it all! I imagine Him up in Heaven with His hands full of provisions, and at the right moment, He provides for our need.

I need to seek God's dream first, and then He will take care of the provision.

Sugar Daddy and a Blesser

Sadly, some of the girls at the universities in South Africa have "sugar daddies" (sometimes the men are even known as "blessers"). These girls will give sex in exchange for financial provision. They sell themselves for new clothes, food, and lovely hairstyles.

These girls have exchanged the truth for a lie. They have sold themselves into slavery. They have allowed the Devil entrance into their lives. Don't sell yourself to the Devil! Trust in God as your Provider. God is the ultimate Blesser.

Sometimes God allows us to go through difficulties. A university student may not have enough food to eat as they try to make a better life for themselves and their family. Someone else may get robbed and lose the laptop that took years to save for. Troubles may come in other areas, like health and relationships.

Maybe it seems that God is not providing for you. You may be asking, "How could God allow such a difficult situation to happen to such a good person?" Despite our trials, we must keep our eyes focused on Jesus and rejoice that He will never abandon us.

The ultimate blessing is that Jesus died on the cross for our sins.

Are you seeking the gift or the Giver of gifts?

If Jesus never gave you another thing, would you still serve Him?

Would you still follow Him because of what He did for you on the cross?

Do You Taste Like Vomit?

Are we like the church in Laodicea? Do we make Jesus want to vomit?

> *I know you inside and out, and find little to my liking. You're not cold, you're not hot—far better to be either cold or hot! You're stale. You're stagnant. You make me want to vomit.* ***You brag, "I'm rich, I've got it made, I need nothing from anyone,"*** *oblivious that in fact you're a pitiful, blind beggar, threadbare and homeless (Revelation 3:15–17, MSG, emphasis added).*

Laodicea relied on their riches to save them instead of God. They thought they had it all, but they were just a pitiful, blind beggar. They had one foot in the world and one foot with God. A true disciple of Christ is "all in" and relies on Jesus for their provision, not in themselves or worldly success. If we don't have both feet on God's side, Jesus will vomit us out of His mouth.

Much like Laodicea, many cultures today have a messed-up concept of being blessed. Many believers think it means being rich, comfortable, and happy.

This becomes a problem when a believer's circumstances fall short of this so-called "blessed life." They struggle to understand why, when they have chosen to obey and follow Christ, they remain poor. Does this mean believers living in the slums of India are not blessed? By no means!

We must be careful when we witness to the lost. The "prosperity gospel" of today has given false promises. The message we bring is that Jesus will save sinners from eternal death, not that He will make us happy and comfortable all the days of our lives. The road of discipleship is often uncomfortable. Many of our blessings will come through sacrifice and trials.

If you are on an airplane and given a parachute to wear, it's important that you know the reason for the parachute. If you are told, "This parachute will make you happy and comfortable," you may be tempted to take it off. It will eventually get heavy, and you may see that others are happy without a parachute. However, if you are told, "This parachute will save your life because the plane is going to crash," you will wear the parachute no matter how uncomfortable it gets. You will keep it on because it will save your life.[5]

Our salvation may get uncomfortable, but it will save our lives. Our salvation is the greatest provision Jesus ever gave us. A real blessing is anything that draws me closer to Jesus.

Ask yourself,

- What am I seeking more than anything else?
- Am I following Christ, expecting earthly gifts of comfort and prosperity to follow?
- Am I seeking Christ because He is the ultimate blessing and worth every sacrifice?
- Are my comforts making me lukewarm, or am I living with ongoing repentance and passion for the gospel of Jesus?

Each of us has to trust in the Dream-Giver to provide. God's provision may not look like you expected. Sometimes a dream takes money, but at other times it simply takes a step of faith.

In reality, it doesn't cost anything to walk up to a stranger and share Jesus with them. It doesn't cost anything to explain a Bible passage to your friend. It will cost you your time. It will cause you to refocus your priorities. Will you choose to follow Jesus?

At the end of the day, know that God is in Heaven with all the provision needed for every dream that is beyond yourself. When the time is right, He will open the floodgates of Heaven and provide so much that you cannot even contain it.

Trust in the Dream-Giver, your Provider.

CHAPTER FIVE
STRIKE!
(GOD, MY PEACE)

*"He makes me lie down in green pastures, he leads me
beside quiet waters, he refreshes my soul."*
—Psalm 23:2–3a

When we work toward our dreams, we can get distracted
by the work and neglect our relationship with God. God
doesn't want us to feel burdened and overwhelmed.
He calls us to cast our cares upon Him and rest in His
peace. He calls us to worship and restore the joy of our
salvation.

September 2, 2010, marked my one-year anniversary in South Africa as a fully-appointed missionary. I
thought of all the things I had done in the past year.
I had run the race—and run hard. But was God proud
of me?

Honestly, my thoughts were, "I'm tired . . . I have nothing left to give . . . can I go on?" I had been doing so much for God that I'd neglected to hear His voice say, "Sarah, I miss you!" Yes, I'd been reading my Bible and praying, but it was more out of duty than love. I had been doing so much to make God known that I had neglected my personal relationship with Him.

We, the church, are the bride of Christ. As a single lady, I often joke that "Jesus is my husband." Well, I had been neglecting Him. He wanted fellowship with me. Most importantly, I needed fellowship with Him.

I felt like God was telling me to "abide" with Him.

The word "abide" means to remain, continue, stay, dwell, reside, and wait for.

The Bible talks about how Jesus is the Vine, and we are the branches. We cannot bear fruit unless we remain in Jesus Christ (John 15:4–5, 9–11, 16). Our strength and joy come from abiding in Him.

How does a branch abide in the Vine? How do we abide in Jesus?

Jesus must be our source of life. All of our nutrients come from the Vine. Nothing comes from us. We are just the branch that brings nutrients from the Vine to the fruit.

> *Remain in me, as I also remain in you. No branch can bear fruit by itself; it must remain in the vine. Neither can you bear fruit unless you remain in me. I am the vine; you are the branches. If you remain in me and I in you, you will bear much fruit; apart from me you can do nothing (John 15:4–5).*

On March 16, 2009, I wrote this in my journal:

> *Today I've been challenged to REMAIN deep in the presence of God. I've not spent enough time with the*

Lord in the past. I must REMAIN in Christ. It is through His Spirit that I will receive strength for the journey. The Lord is calling me to go deeper. He doesn't just have a call on my life but a mandate. . . . I need to get on my knees in prayer. The Lord's sheep know His voice. I need to hear the whisper of His voice. The Enemy will attack—I must have the armor of God and the Spirit to stand. . . .

There is a theme in everyone's life—it's you and Jesus, Jesus and you! God desires a love story between you and Him. Let's stop and smell the roses. This world is so busy! Are we too busy to spend time with Jesus? If so, then we are too busy. Psalm 6:10 says, "Be still and know that I am God." Will we quiet ourselves and make time to know God? Will we abide in Christ?

There is a theme in everyone's life — it's you and Jesus, Jesus and you!

How Do We Abide in Christ?

"God is love. Whoever lives in love lives in God, and God in them."
—1 John 4:16b

We abide by loving.

We are called to remain in the Father's love. When someone is "in love," it produces joy in their lives. They just can't stop smiling. If you feel tired and burdened, God's love will bring you peace.

As the Father has loved me, so have I loved you. Now **remain** *in my love.* **If you keep** *my commands,* **you** *will remain in my love, just as I have kept my Father's commands and remain in his love. I have told you this so that my **joy** may be in you and that your **joy** may be complete. . . . You did not choose me, but I chose you and appointed you so that you might go and bear fruit—**fruit that will last**—and so that **whatever you ask in my name the Father will give you** (John 15:9–11, 16, emphasis added).*

We abide by obeying.

Obedience is not always about doing "good works." God also calls us to prayer and worship. If you do not abide in Christ, your branch will soon die. When people tell me they are losing faith, the first question I ask is "Are you praying and reading your Bible?" Most often the answer is no. The person has stopped abiding, so their branch has started dying.

Obedience is bending our will to God's will. To know God's will, you must spend time with Him.

"But if anyone obeys his word, love for God is truly made complete in them. This is how we know we are in him: Whoever claims to live in him must live as Jesus did" (1 John 2:5–6).

We abide by waiting.

If we pay attention to the way Jesus lived, we will see that there were times when He performed miracles and preached sermons to thousands of people. But there were also days when He took the time to be alone with God. Jesus stopped the "busyness" and waited to hear from the Father. "But Jesus often withdrew to lonely places and prayed" (Luke 5:16).

Do you take time out of your day to wait on God and hear from Him? Or is God saying, "I miss you"?

Waiting implies attentiveness, listening, and expectation. We must set aside time to hear from God and expect His reply.

"Show me Your ways, O Lord; teach me Your paths. Lead me in Your truth and teach me, for You are the God of my salvation; on You I *wait* all the day" (Psalm 25:4–5, NKJV, emphasis added).

We expectantly wait for God's presence in the same way that we wait in the doctor's office. We know the doctor can help us. He cares about us. He will address our needs.

Waiting develops patience, perseverance, and faithfulness. We trust in God through hard times. Even when the answer doesn't come right away, we must not give up. We continue to remain in Christ while waiting on Him. We are dependent on Christ like the branch is dependent on the vine. Jesus is the Bread of life—He is our nourishment.

God is calling us to abide in Him. We abide because we love Him. We abide because we desire to obey Him. As we abide, we wait upon Him. This is when we know the peace of God.

Do you set aside a time to pray every day?

"But you, when you pray, go into your room, and when you have shut your door, pray to your Father who is in the secret place; and your Father who sees in secret will reward you openly" (Matthew 6:6).

You are as close to Jesus as you choose to be. It's your choice. Will you love, obey, and wait on God? If you want to go deep into His presence, then you must stay connected to the Vine.

Being vs. Doing

"He makes me lie down in green pastures, he leads me beside quiet waters, he restores my soul."
—Psalm 23:2–3a

The fact that we are busy does not mean that we are doing what God wants us to do. We can be living in disobedience even while doing "ministry." Sometimes we have to say no to *good* things to say yes to *God* things.

When we become weary in doing good, it is because we are not sitting at Jesus' feet daily. We need to spend time with God and meditate on His Word every day. Then it will be exciting to do God's work—not tiring. He will be our strength.

If you don't want to get stressed out, *pray every day*! Take time to sit at Jesus' feet.

The story of Mary and Martha is the classic example of being vs. doing. Mary enjoyed "being" in Jesus' presence while Martha was too busy "doing" things for Him.

As Jesus and his disciples were on their way, he came to a village where a woman named Martha opened her home to him. She had a sister called Mary, who sat at the Lord's feet listening to what he said. But Martha was distracted by all the preparations that had to be made. She came to him and asked, "Lord, don't you care that my sister has left me to do the work by myself? Tell her to help me!"

"Martha, Martha," the Lord answered, "you are worried and upset about many things, but few things are needed—or indeed only one. Mary has chosen what is better, and it will not be taken away from her" (Luke 10:38–42).

My personality is like Martha's. I enjoy working and getting things done. If I'm working hard and someone else is just standing around talking to someone, I can feel a little upset and neglected. When I feel this way, I need to check my attitude.

Dreaming beyond yourself was never meant to be a heavy burden. Jesus' burden is light. It becomes heavy when we try to do things in our own strength instead of through God. We should never neglect sitting at Jesus' feet. Don't worry about all the work that needs to be done. If it's God's dream, then He will help you accomplish it.

Load Shedding

In the year 2015, South Africa experienced something called "load shedding." The demand for electricity was greater than the supply, so it was shut off at certain times of day to conserve power.

For some reason, when I lived in America, I thought the supply of electricity was "endless." Maybe it would be interrupted by an ice storm or accident, but I knew that the electricity would soon be back on.

This experience of load shedding has taught me that sometimes you need to take a break and conserve energy so that you will have enough to give when you need it.

Our power source is God. "My message and my preaching were not with wise and persuasive words, but with a demonstration of the Spirit's power, so that your faith might not rest on human wisdom, but on God's power" (1 Corinthians 2:4–5).

We need God's power to light up our dark days. When people look at me, they should be able to recognize God's power living in me.

It's amazing how many distractions are eliminated from your life when the electricity turns off. You can't plug into your TV, computer, or cell phone. Sometimes, we need to unplug from distractions and plug into the ultimate power source—God.

One of the Ten Commandments is to take a Sabbath rest (Exodus 20:8). God has commanded us to rest in His presence. If I need a time of rest or peace in my life, I have to write the word "booked" on my calendar. This allows me to tell people that I'm already "booked" on that day or time. (Now you know my secret.) As a pastor, Sunday is a work day for me, not a rest day. If I don't find rest in my week, I will soon burn out and be good for no one.

Setting aside time for Jesus shouldn't happen just one day a week. I need to make a habit to schedule a personal devotional time with Jesus. You may think that putting Jesus on your calendar is limiting God. Shouldn't Jesus have our entire day? We do need to leave room in our lives for godly interruptions, but I also recognize that if we don't set a time and place for personal devotion, it may not happen at all.

On April 22, 2013, I wrote about scheduling a "Holy Spirit Date Night":

> *God is calling me back to remaining in Him. John 15:5 says, "I am the vine, you are the branches. If you remain in me and I in you, you will bear much fruit; apart from me you can do nothing." I don't need to focus on **doing** and **bearing fruit** but rather focus on **becoming** closer to Jesus and **remaining** in Him.*
>
> *The past month God has challenged me to take one night of the week and designate it as my "Holy Spirit*

Date Night." As a result, I've grown closer to Him. All that is asked of me as a missionary is too much to bear alone. I can only do it through Jesus. God encouraged me with this word:

"I am your strong tower, the shelter over you. My grace is sufficient; My power in and through you is the same power that raised Christ from the dead."

My relationship with the Lord is more important than anything else. If I have to say 'no' to doing a mission service so I can spend time with Jesus—I will. Even Jesus had to take time to go to lonely places and pray.

Lord, thank You that You are my strong tower, You are my shelter—and I run to You. Thank You for Your grace in the midst of this fallen world. Thank You for empowering me with the Holy Spirit. Through You all things are possible! You are victorious over the grave! You have defeated Satan. I am on the winning team. I rest in Your shelter. I trust in You for the journey ahead.

Are you setting aside time to be with Jesus? Are you load shedding? Will you turn off the distractions so you can focus on renewing your power source?

Can I Just Eat Some Ice Cream?

Do you have "high stress" moments? There are days when I feel overwhelmed by the task before me. But shouldn't I be living in peace? Why should I be stressed out? At these times, I have to slow myself down and recognize that I need to sit at Jesus' feet. Jesus always makes everything better!

"Therefore, since we have been justified through faith, we have *peace* with God through the Lord Jesus Christ. . . ." (Romans 5:1, emphasis added).

"And he will be called Wonderful Counselor, Mighty

God, Everlasting Father, *Prince of Peace*" (Isaiah 9:6b, emphasis added).

Even the prophet Elijah had some high-stress moments. Out of obedience to God, he had prayed that there would be no rain. The problem was that this resulted in a famine. But God provided for Elijah's needs with a brook to drink from and ravens that brought him bread and meat. When the brook dried up, God performed another miracle by providing for Elijah through the widow of Zarephath. God always met his needs (1 Kings 17).

Then Elijah had his epic moment on Mount Carmel when all the prophets of Baal were defeated, and Elijah proved that his God was the only true God (1 Kings 18).

But in 1 Kings 19, Elijah was running for his life because Jezebel wanted to kill him. Elijah even prayed, "I have had enough Lord. Take my life . . ." (v. 4). However, God didn't abandon him. He sent an angel to attend to him because he would need supernatural strength for the journey ahead.

Elijah was extremely discouraged. He felt like a failure. But how could he after such an amazing victory over the prophets of Baal? Elijah was discouraged because his purpose was to bring people back to God. The real victory would have been for the prophets and Jezebel to turn back to God. Instead, Jezebel wanted to kill Elijah. Elijah also felt like he was all alone in standing up for God's truth (v. 10), and he was physically exhausted from a long journey (vv. 3–4).

God deals with our discouragement as He did with Elijah's: in an understanding and caring way. First of all, God allowed Elijah to sleep (vv. 5–6). Sometimes the most spiritual thing you can do is take a nap! Some people may give you a hard time for falling asleep when you are praying (and I wouldn't make this a habit), but there are times when God's answer to your prayers is physical rest.

When we are discouraged, sometimes our physical bodies just need proper food. God provided Elijah with food to eat (vv. 5–7). I'll admit that sometimes when I'm discouraged, I like to eat a bowl of ice cream. In my discouragement, I should always seek God first, and I don't want to make food an idol. However, a good meal can bring strength back to your body. I'm not sure if ice cream counts as a good meal, but let's be real here—ice creams sounds good when you've had a bad day!

In Elijah's frustration, God spoke to him—not in a loud way but a gentle whisper (vv. 11–13). God will also speak to us and reveal His power and presence. He will give us direction for the next step we should take (vv. 15–18). And He will not leave us alone on the journey; just as God gave Elisha to Elijah, He will bring people with encouraging spirits into our lives (vv. 16, 19–21).

When you get discouraged and want to quit pursuing God's dream for your life, know that you can depend on God to give you strength, help, and encouragement. You can also trust that He will equip you with what you need to complete His dream.

To encourage and strengthen Elijah's faith, God visited him on Mount Horeb. Sometimes, when you find yourself in a desperate situation, you look for God to show up in an extraordinary way. What you need to do is get alone with God and quiet yourself. Take your mind off of the distractions and allow God to speak His gentle peace into your life.

"As a father has compassion on his children, so the Lord has compassion on those who fear him; for he knows how we are formed, he remembers that we are dust" (Psalm 103:13–14).

God has compassion on us because He knows our weaknesses. He sees us when we fail or suffer. He hurts when we hurt. God is not distant or uncaring. Remember that He looks on us with compassion and will help us with whatever we need.

Strike!

When I was growing up in America, an unscheduled day off from school usually happened because of snow. The roads were too dangerous to drive on, so we were given a "snow day." In South Africa, there is no snow, but I still get random days off from working with university students. I call them "strike days."

At the poorer universities that cater almost exclusively to black Africans, students have been protesting against rising fees and the cost of higher education since 1994. Some of these strikes are not peaceful. Buses and school buildings have been burned. Though the students want a degree, they choose to stop attending classes and strike to get the attention of the administration and government. Everything stops so that the leadership will listen.

These strikes relate to our relationship with God in two ways.

First of all, when God is in our lives, He brings peace—not destruction. Many students are trying to make their demands peacefully, but often outsiders come in, or a few destructive students make everyone else look bad. It doesn't make sense to destroy school property when you are asking for financial aid. The schools have to spend more money to fix what was destroyed rather than use those funds to help the situation.

Jesus came as a Wonderful Counselor and Prince of Peace. He can calm every situation and answer every need. God's love will bring peace in our lives. I'm not sure if there is a "godly" strike. If there is, it doesn't involve tear gas or burning buses. If we are walking with the Prince of Peace, our actions will also bring peace to each situation we face.

Secondly, we should be so desperate for an answer from the higher power that we are willing to stop everything and take a risk to get attention. Are we as desperate to hear from God as these students are to have their demands heard? Would we be willing to "strike" our average lives and take a risk to get different results?

There are days when I want to strike. I'm frustrated with life as it is. Something needs to change.

What needs to change in your life? Are there bad habits you need to break? Do you need to take some time off to seek the Lord for an answer?

Africa, the Musical

When you are having a bad day, do you ever turn on worship music? If you choose to sing along and praise God, the problems and cares often fade away. You will begin to feel the peace of God flood over you. It's amazing how worship can change things. We stop focusing on ourselves, and we start focusing on how amazing our God is.

Growing up, I always loved musicals. In the middle of a conversation or any menial task, someone may put their mood into music. One of my favorite musicals is "Singing in the Rain." Despite the weather, actor Gene Kelly joyfully dances through the streets while singing. There is a sense of freedom in not caring what other people think of you and expressing your joy through song and dance!

One reason I love Africa so much is that it's like a musical come to life. Finally, I get to be a part of the musical *Live*! As a teenager, I could barely raise my hands in worship or even "jump" in a song. Now I can't seem to stop my feet from moving!

2 Samuel 6:14 says, "David was dancing before the Lord with all his might. . . ." When others didn't approve, he responded in verse 22, "I will become even more undignified than this, and I will be humiliated in my own eyes."

Africa has shown me the freedom and joy of worshiping the Lord in song and *dance*! The awesome thing about the African people is that they don't care that I'm not always on the beat! They just love that I join them in their freedom of worship.

Don't allow the fear of what others will think of you stop you from worshiping the Lord! Let's humble ourselves! Let's get a little undignified!

At one event in South Africa, youth gathered together for what they called a "Worship Explosion." I was chosen as the guest speaker for the day. When they first asked me to speak, I honestly thought they had the wrong person. I was not a "worship leader." I don't sing solos or play any instrument. Then God showed me that you don't have to sing well or play an instrument to lead others in true worship.

"Yet a time is coming and has now come when the true worshipers will worship the Father in the Spirit and in truth, for they are the kind of worshipers the Father seeks" (John 4:23).

The Samaritan woman in John 4 wasn't worshiping God with her life but was going through the formalities of religion. She was not living in the peace of God.

How many of us just go through the formalities but don't worship God with our lives? Real worship involves obedience. The Samaritan woman may have been "worshiping" God, but she wasn't living her life in devotion to Him.

Worship is more than singing words to a few slow songs. Worship is about living the lyrics.

When you live the lyrics, you will know the peace of God.

CHAPTER SIX
LADYBUGS
(GOD, MY FATHER)

The Spirit you received does not make you slaves,
so that you live in fear again; rather, the Spirit you
received brought about your adoption to sonship.
And by him we cry, "Abba, Father."
—Romans 8:15

Have you ever felt like your dream has crashed or gotten stuck in the mud?

Don't give up. Your heavenly Father has not abandoned you. He cares for you and loves you. Look beyond the situation to the love of your Father.

September 11, 2001, was the day when the World Trade Center Towers were attacked, and so many people lost their family members and friends. The entire world watched as this great tragedy unfolded.

September 12, 2001, was significant to me because I experienced my own small "tragedy." While driving home from school, I became distracted and lost control of my car.

There had been a ladybug crawling on my driver's side window. Rather than ignoring it, I decided to flick the ladybug out the window. At the same time, I was driving around a sharp curve too fast.

Somehow, I got slightly off the road and onto the gravel shoulder. As I was an inexperienced driver, this scared me so much that I overcorrected the vehicle. My car rolled over and back onto its wheels, facing the opposite direction.

There was a trucking company across the road. Some of the employees must have heard or seen the crash. They rushed over to help me get out of the vehicle and called 911.

I remember pulling a piece of windshield glass out of my hand after the accident. A week later, I went to the doctor to have more glass dug out. Other than that, I seemed to be fine.

I knew I needed to tell my parents what had happened. This was before cell phones were popular, so I borrowed one from someone to call my mom who was working as a church secretary. No one answered. The policeman came to question me, so I set the phone down next to me. The policeman asked me a lot of questions, which I answered honestly, even admitting that a ladybug had been the cause of the accident. I found out later that I'd forgotten to end the call on the church phone. My entire conversation with the police officer was recorded on the church answering machine!

Because of the state of my car, I was taken to the nearest hospital in an ambulance. I remember my parents coming into the room and seeing my dad crying. My dad was never one to tell me that he loved me or pull me up on his lap when I was a child. His tears shocked me. I kept saying, "I'm sorry about the car." But my dad replied, "The car can be replaced. I'm just glad you are okay." I remember thinking, "My dad does love me?" (Since that day, my dad has grown a lot. Almost every time we talk he says, "I love you," and he loves holding his grandchildren on his lap. All of us are a work in progress. I'm thankful for my father's love.)

The next day, the local newspaper featured my story. Of course, the front page featured the terrorist attacks on the World Trade Center, but the second page said, "Teen Hurt While Swatting Ladybug off of Windshield." The fact that I totaled my car because of a ladybug has haunted me for years. My senior yearbook is full of students and teachers saying, "Watch out for the ladybugs!"

I'm thankful that God spared my life that day. He wasn't finished with me.

That was also the day when I recognized that my earthly father loved me. I don't know what your relationship with your earthly father has been. Maybe you've never met him. Maybe he was incredible. Maybe he wasn't a good dad.

Our perception of our heavenly Father should not become distorted because of a flawed earthly father. God loves us very much. We are His sons and daughters. He cares about every detail of our lives. When we hurt, He cries.

> Our perception of our heavenly Father should not become distorted because of a flawed earthly father.

The truth is that He has always loved us. Sometimes it takes a difficult situation to open our eyes so we can see the Father's love.

Tires, Trailers, and Tiaras

As a child, I would classify myself as a "momma's girl." I loved being in the kitchen helping my mom cook a meal for our family of six. The smell of freshly baked chocolate chip cookies, apple pie, or banana bread is a reminder of wonderful times spent with my mother.

Since there were four children in our family—two girls and two boys—the boys often went places with Dad, and the girls stayed with Mom. At the time, I didn't mind. Why would I want to learn how to work on a car or take trips to the hardware store? I was happy in the kitchen with Mom. I was the "princess" and didn't care about getting dirty with my dad.

As soon as I arrived in Africa as a single missionary, I realized that some of those lessons might have been helpful. After my first short trip to Africa, I asked my father to teach me how to change oil and a flat tire. He had always done these things for me. He loved me and made sure my car was in working order, but he wouldn't be in Africa. Because I asked, my father lovingly took the time to teach me the skills of car repair and maintenance.

My brothers grew up driving tractors and pulling trailers. Again, I had never cared to learn. In Africa, I would have to drive a manual transmission and reverse a trailer. Again, I asked my father. For about a month, he taught me how to change gears and not stall in the middle of an intersection. Another summer, he and my brother Chad also took the time to help me reverse a trailer (for what seemed like hundreds of times) until I learned.

These experiences taught me that we learn from spending time with our Father. We learn even more when we ask for His help! He loves us and will look out for our wellbeing. God wants us to ask Him to teach us like I asked my Dad for help changing a tire. He doesn't want to force Himself on us. He desires to be there for us, but we must welcome Him to do so.

Shipwrecked

At one point in his missionary journeys, the Apostle Paul had been experiencing fruitful ministry. However, he felt that God was leading him to go to Jerusalem, the most dangerous place for him (Acts 21). Many of the other believers warned him not to go. But Paul said, "I am ready not only to be bound, but also to die in Jerusalem for the name of the Lord Jesus" (Acts 21:13b).

Paul saw his trials as opportunities for him to speak the truth of Jesus. He used every circumstance to share Jesus with the lost, from the lowest class of people to the most important authorities. King Agrippa said to Paul, "Do you think that in such a short time you can persuade me to be a Christian?" (Acts 26:28). Paul replied, "Short time or long—I pray to God that not only you but all who are listening to me today may become what I am, except for these chains" (v. 29).

By birth, Paul was a Roman citizen. This gave him the right to a fair trial. He could have been released if he had not appealed to Caesar, but it seemed that Paul had a calling to not only proclaim the gospel to the high officials in Jerusalem but also to Caesar himself.

Eventually, Paul was put on a ship to Rome. In Paul's mind, he was on an all-expenses-paid missionary trip to Rome at the government's expense! Paul saw his chains as an opportunity to proclaim the message of Jesus to those he wouldn't have been able to otherwise. He obediently represented Christ wherever he went and in every situation.

Paul knew that he had a heavenly Father who cared deeply for him and would always be with him—no matter how difficult the situation. God the Father encouraged Paul not to be afraid. God's dream would be fulfilled in His life.

> *Last night an angel of the God to whom I belong and whom I serve stood beside me and said, "Do not be afraid, Paul. You must stand trial before Caesar; and God has graciously given you the lives of all who sail with you." So keep up your courage, men, for I have faith in God that it will happen just as he told me (Acts 27:23–25).*

Paul's vessel was shipwrecked, but not one person died. This was a testimony to every sailor and soldier on the ship that Paul's God was real. God even had a plan about where they would be shipwrecked—the island of Malta. The people of Malta also needed to believe in Jesus.

While building a fire on the island, Paul was bitten by a poisonous snake. The people expected him to die, thinking that he must have done something terrible to deserve such punishment. But when nothing happened to him, they assumed that Paul was a god (Acts 28:2–6). This incident gave Paul an invitation to the chief official's home. When Paul prayed for the official's father who was sick in bed, the man was healed. The rest of the sick on the island came to him and were cured. These miracles allowed Paul to share about the one true God. God's dream of saving people continued to be fulfilled even through Paul's trials.

> *Go into all the world and preach the gospel to all creation. Whoever believes and is baptized will be saved, but whoever does not believe will be condemned. And*

these signs will accompany those who believe: In my name they will drive out demons; they will speak in new tongues; they will pick up snakes with their hands; and when they drink deadly poison, it will not hurt them at all; they will place their hands on sick people, and they will get well (Mark 16:15–18).

In Africa, some false teachers are trying to demonstrate the power of God. They have people drink petrol to prove that "if you drink anything poisonous it won't harm you." However, God didn't call us to drink poison on purpose. He never told us to go to the local zoo and stand in the snake pit to prove that God is real. What father would tell his child to do that? Our heavenly Father is a good father. He doesn't ask his children to be stupid. This false theology misrepresents the Father's love. It makes non-believers turn away from God instead of toward Him.

Our Father loves us and desires to see us fulfill dreams beyond ourselves. As we go about this work, He says not to worry because He will be with you! We live in a fallen world with a spiritual battle going on. We may encounter demonic forces, but God will be with us. Someone or something may try to harm us, but the Father is with us! When someone is sick, the Father will heal them. Believers are called to pray in faith, but the Father does the work. We can't take the credit.

Many times, our trials are actually platforms for us to proclaim the goodness of our heavenly Father. Jesus had to die on a cross. The Father knew that this was the only way for the human race to be redeemed. The Father allowed his Son to suffer so that we could also become His children.

Many times, our trials are actually platforms for us to proclaim the goodness of our heavenly Father.

The book of Acts ends with Paul being held under Roman guard. The last verse says, "He proclaimed the kingdom of God and taught about the Lord Jesus Christ—with all boldness and without hindrance!" (Acts 28:31). Don't let your trials stop you from boldly proclaiming Jesus to everyone you encounter.

Maybe you feel like your faith has been shipwrecked. How could a loving Father allow you to go through such a painful trial? We won't understand some things until we reach Heaven. Maybe you feel like God has abandoned you. This is a lie from Satan. God has not left you. Your heavenly Father loves you. He wants to hold you and comfort you. Reach out to your Father today. He is waiting.

The Father has a dream for your life. You are still alive! He's not done with you. Make the most of the journey. You are not alone. He is with you.

Are you using your trials as platforms to share the Father's love with others?

Are you willing to do whatever it takes to see God's dreams fulfilled?

Stuck in the Mud

One Saturday in December 2010, my friends and I ministered to the youth of a small church in the mountainous Venda region of South Africa. During the rainy season, the dirt roads turn into mud and can be very dangerous. These mountain roads have no guardrails, and if a vehicle slides, it could fall right off the edge of a small cliff and onto the houses below.

That morning, rather than risk getting stuck in the mud, the pastor of the local church recommended that we park at the bottom of the mountain and take a 30-minute hike up. We held a service in the morning, and during the afternoon, I taught on how to be a witness. We then went out in groups to evangelize the village. We saw five people give their hearts to God! The sun shone all day, and the ground was dry, so the pastor assured me that the next day I could drive up the mountain.

As I woke up Sunday morning to the sound of monkeys running on the roof, I thought I also heard a slight drizzle of rain. I called the pastor to see if we should walk up the mountain again, but he assured me that the roads were fine. As I drove to the bottom of the mountain, the drizzle of rain continued. I called him again, and he assured me that I would be all right. My Toyota Fortuner started climbing the mountain.

We eventually came to a very steep hill. About halfway up, my tires started spinning. I could go no further. My friends said, "Sarah, are you okay?" In a panicked voice, I replied, "Does it look like I'm okay?" I let the car roll slowly back down the incline. Rather than reversing the entire way down, I pulled into the driveway of someone's house. As I tried to get back onto the road, my car slipped and slid. I was stuck.

Soon the house's residents came out to see what all the noise was. They were some of the youth from the church. I was thankful that we were stuck at a friend's house. They tried pushing the car, but it didn't work. I decided to leave the car, walk to the church, and pray the rain would stop. That was our only hope of getting down the mountain.

I had several Bibles in the Venda language to give away, so I unloaded the car and packed my bag full of Bibles. My hands were too full for an umbrella, so I chose to let the rain fall on me. We walked over the large hill that I had just slid down.

When we arrived at the church, the rain only grew stronger. I kept praying that the rain would stop, but it only poured more and more. The sound of rain on the church's metal roof echoed in my ears. I thought we were going to be stuck on the mountain for days and would have to sleep in the village.

During the service, there was a devotion on Paul and Silas in prison. They praised God instead of dwelling on their problems. I tried my best to thank God and praise Him as I watched the rain fall from the sky. Thankfully, my friend preached the Sunday sermon. Throughout the entire message, I continued to pray that the rains would stop.

During the altar call, I went up to pray for other people. Then the rain stopped! When I quit focusing on myself, my prayers were answered. The sun began to shine again. Remembering the Bibles I had carried up the mountain, I gave them to those who didn't have a Bible. Miraculously, I had grabbed the exact number needed.

After church, we ate with the pastor and his family, and then we made our way to the car. This pastor had eight sons. A few of the older sons and the pastor helped push the car out of the mud. It was still slipping and sliding all over, wheels spinning. Miraculously, I made it out of the driveway.

We said our goodbyes and prayerfully headed down the mountain. At one point the car started to slide in the mud. My stomach turned as I guided the steering wheel toward the safety of the path. I was so relieved when we reached the tar road.

That was not the end of the story. It had a sequel. . . .

The following year—at the same time, the rainy season—I was asked to assist missionaries Wayne and Delight Peercy with a Christmas project in Venda. We were able to bring food parcels and gifts to 94 families and orphans affected by HIV/AIDS. The forecast was clear skies for day one, but the next day there was an 80 percent chance of rain. Honestly, I didn't want to face those mountains again.

Thankfully, God gave me the following Scripture passage during my morning devotions.

> *I lift up my eyes to the mountains—where does my help come from? My help comes from the Lord, the Maker of heaven and earth. . . . The Lord will keep you from all harm—he will watch over your life; the Lord will watch over your coming and going both now and forevermore (Psalm 121:1–2, 7–8).*

The words in this Psalm seemed to leap off the page as if God Himself were speaking to me. As a result, I faced the mountain full of faith that God—the creator of the mountain and the rains—would watch over me and help me get up the mountain and *down it*! Indeed, this is what God did.

As I was driving back to Pretoria the following day, the heavens opened and unleashed a powerful rainstorm. Thankfulness filled my heart. God had held the rain back and kept the mountain dry so we could reach the people of Venda with the gift of Jesus and God's love.

Our heavenly Father will often allow us to go through the rains of life. We may even get stuck in the mud. Do you feel like your dream is stuck in the mud today? Rest assured that God sees your coming and going! Don't get so focused on the problem that you neglect to pray for others and keep your focus on your heavenly Father.

Sometimes He lets the rains come. Other times He stops them. We have to trust that our Father knows what we can handle. He knows the past, present, and future. He wants the dream to come true. We may need to get a little dirty before we see the sunshine.

Am I in Trouble?

As the second born of four children, my personality was that of a peacemaker. I only recall a few times when I was disciplined by my earthly father. One of them was shortly after my mom had gallbladder surgery. My sister and I were upstairs in our house. For some reason, she had thought it would be an adventure to climb out the window onto the roof of the house. (My sister remembers some of this story a little differently than I do—but I'm the one writing this book, so you get to hear what I "chose" to remember. Let's just say we were both guilty.)

Our windows had screens on them, so we carefully removed them, and she climbed out onto the roof of our family home. This scared me, so I didn't venture out but called from the window for my sister to come back inside. Just then my aunt drove by. We prayed that she didn't see us. But she had and pulled into our driveway.

My sister quickly squeezed back through the window. We tried to put the screen back, but in our panicked state, it was impossible. We abandoned the evidence and hid under our parents' bed.

My mom found us and tried her best to discipline us. However, as she was weak from her surgery, she said the words that every child fears, "Just wait until your father gets home." She made us wait in our bedroom the rest of the afternoon.

We had a lot of time to prepare ourselves for our father's eminent arrival. Though today it may be looked down upon, my parents still believed in spanking. We knew this was coming, so we devised a plan. We put on several pairs of underwear and stuffed a blanket down the backs of our pants to alleviate the impact of the spank upon our backsides.

When my father finally did come home, he soon made his way to our room. Today I wonder how he contained his laughter when he saw our extra-large backsides. He pulled out the blankets and gave us a spanking.

> *Endure hardship as discipline; God is treating you as his children. For what children are not disciplined by their father? . . . No discipline seems pleasant at the time, but painful. Later on, however, it produces a harvest of righteousness and peace for those who have been trained by it (Hebrews 12:7, 11).*

Hardships are the training ground for righteousness and peace. If we are God's children, we will be disciplined. He corrects those He loves (Hebrews 12:6). My earthly father loved us. He didn't want his daughters falling off the roof of the house! He needed to discipline us to protect us from harm.

No discipline is pleasant at the time. Now I look back and am thankful for my father's correction. I even laugh at the blankets stuffed into our pants! God used this experience to teach my sister and me to stay off the roof of the house. The Lord loves us and desires for each of His children to live out their God-given potential. Sometimes He has to train us and smooth out our rough patches, polishing us until we are ready to be used by Him.

Stuck in the Sand

Living in Africa has taught me to overcome every fear and obstacle in the power of Jesus Christ. In 2012, I was able to travel with some other South African missionaries to the country of Botswana to minister to the youth and partner with their local missionaries. We arrived a day before the ministry began to enjoy a drive through the Khama Rhino Sanctuary.

The sandy soil put my missionary vehicle to the test once again. In one particular spot, it got stuck. Unfortunately, I do not have four-wheel drive, only a locking differential. (If you don't know what that is, you can google it, but it basically means that both wheels on the axle lock together.) We attempted to use the diff lock, but the car was so stuck in the sand that it seemed hopeless. Thankfully, the Botswana army patrols that area for Rhino poachers. The soldiers saw our need and stopped to help push me out. From then on, I tried to avoid the very sandy places.

When we had to go back down the same road, I finally decided to face my fears. As we approached the sand, I gave my vehicle gas and made my way through safely. For the rest of the day, I actually found it exciting to drive through the sandy areas. I enjoyed the challenge. The other missionaries agreed that I had found a new love for "off-roading."

"Off-roading" is something my father and brothers loved to do when I was young. I had disliked it because I was always the "whiplashed" passenger. They never let me drive. Now that I had faced my fears of driving in the sand, I realized I loved it.

Throughout our lives, there may be moments when we seem to get "stuck in the sand." Thankfully, our heavenly Father will always provide a way out—if we will only ask Him for assistance. He sent me an army!

Our past failures should not stop us from facing our fears and going where God has called us to go. We may be surprised to find that God's path is the grand adventure that we have longed to experience.

Our Father wants us to enjoy fulfilling the dream. He doesn't want us to walk in fear or spiritual heaviness. He will laugh with us as we ride through the sand and enjoy the bumps along the way. He also teaches us how to use the diff lock. When it doesn't work, He sends the army to help us. There is no need to fear the road ahead because our Father is in the vehicle. He is on the journey with us.

If we have fallen or gotten stuck in the mud or sand, let's learn from our mistakes and keep moving ahead. We have not "failed." We have only hit a pothole in the road. Our Father loves us and wants to see us graduate to trusting in Him so we can enjoy the adventure.

Trust the Dream-Giver—God, your Father.

CHAPTER SEVEN
VAMPIRES
(GOD, MY DEFENDER)

For our struggle is not against flesh and blood,
but against the rulers, against the authorities,
against the powers of this dark world and against
the spiritual forces of evil in the heavenly realms.
—Ephesians 6:12

When you pursue God's dream, you make the Devil mad at you.

The Devil was already upset over losing you to Christ. It seems that he is content as long as you stay a nominal Christian. The Devil doesn't mind if you go to church on Sundays and read your Bible. However, the Devil gets very nervous when you start making God's dreams come true.

Does the Devil know your name? What is his opinion

of you? The evil spirit in Acts 19:15 said, "Jesus I know, and Paul I know about, but who are you?" If you are fighting for God's dreams, the Devil will start paying attention to your name.

Satan knows that you have the potential to impact many lost souls for eternity. Once you start stepping out in faith, you will face opposition from the Enemy. The Devil will try to discourage you from accomplishing God's dreams. At first, you may feel that you are doing something wrong. "If I'm accomplishing God's will, why is it so difficult?" We must remember that we are in a battle.

A spiritual battle is taking place in the heavenly realms. Our fight is not against other people. It's against our Enemy, the Devil. The good news is that we are on the winning team! We know how the battle ends— God wins!

In today's culture, it seems that we've downplayed spiritual warfare so that it's just something on television or in a movie theater. Our culture has become desensitized to the reality of the spiritual battles we face in our everyday lives.

Vampires and Birthday Parties

While I was pushing my nephew on the swing at a local park, I overheard two other children arguing over "red" or "black." Finally, another girl slightly older than them came over and asked why they were fighting. One replied, "I want red vampire eyes, but she wants black vampire eyes." The older girl said, "Look. You can both be vampires. You have black eyes, and you have red eyes!"

A vampire, by definition, is a corpse which has left its grave to drink the blood of the living by biting their necks with long pointed canine teeth.[6]

This incident in the park shocked me. How can innocent children play vampires? Somehow their parents must have allowed the media to teach them that evil is good.

You might think I'm overreacting, but I believe that we have lost our perception of what is wrong. 1 Peter 5:8 says that Satan "prowls around like a roaring lion looking for someone to devour." Are we allowing the Enemy to consume us?

In South Africa, my eyes were opened to the reality of spiritual warfare. At almost every youth camp or youth rally, a young person would manifest a demonic spirit and need deliverance. Witchcraft and demonic powers were very real. You don't have to convince an African that there is a spiritual world.

The demonic realm is out in the open in Africa, but just because it hides in other countries does not mean that it is not there.

In the United States, it seems that our children and many adults think the spirit world is a story or fairy tale. However, I can tell you that the spirit world is very real! There is a Heaven, and there is a Hell. There is a God, and there is a Devil. There are angels, and there are demons.

Why would we want to welcome the Devil into our lives?

Why would we want to play with the Enemy?

My birthday is on October 31, Halloween. In American culture, Halloween is a time where kids dress up and get free candy. Who doesn't want free candy? As a small child, we put on Halloween costumes and visited our family on the 30th so that we could celebrate my birthday on the 31st.

Later, as my family became more involved in church activities, we volunteered at the church "Harvest Party," the Christian alternative to Halloween. This church event allowed children to have fun in a safe way. It also allowed the church to reach out to nonbelievers in the community. When there is darkness in the world, we should always look for ways we can bring the light of Jesus.

Because my birthday was on Halloween, I always felt like I shared my birthday with the Devil's holiday. Though some parts of Halloween remain innocent, other parts welcome demons. When I was a child, we came home from church at Halloween time to find that someone had thrown eggs at our home, put toilet paper in our trees, and killed our dog by hanging him in our apple tree. These "pranksters" were not just having fun by joking with us. This was demonic because they killed our family pet. I remember crying as I blew out the candles on my birthday cake and sobbing, "How can I have a good birthday when they killed our dog?"

For Halloween, many children and adults dress up as witches, zombies, vampires, and other disturbing characters. Society invites us to play with demonic forces. Do we recognize the reality of the spiritual realm?

Knowing the truth about spiritual warfare could cause some people to walk in fear that the Devil is out to get them. If you have Christ in your life, you don't need to walk in fear. The Holy Spirit that is living in you is greater than the one who is in the world (1 John 4:4). We can overcome the enemy by the blood of the Lamb (Jesus) and the word of our testimony (Revelation 12:11).

Jesus already won the battle over the Devil on the cross. He has not left us alone—He's given us the Holy Spirit. We are overcomers!

Perhaps you feel that you have allowed the Enemy to come into your home or life. Do you sense that you are in spiritual darkness? Maybe you feel as though you've lost something of great value.

"Or suppose a woman has ten silver coins and loses one. Doesn't she light a lamp, sweep the house and search carefully until she finds it?" (Luke 15:8).

Why did the woman need to light the lamp? She had allowed the light to go out. Her house was dark! Jesus Christ is the Light of the World. Have we allowed the Light to go out in our homes?

Why did she need to clean her house? She had allowed it to get dirty. Have we allowed the dirt of the world to come into our homes?[7]

My prayer is that we would relight the lamp of Jesus Christ in our homes and clean out the filth of the world so that we might find that which is of great value.

I also pray that we would recognize the spiritual battle around us. Let us take our stand "against the devil's schemes" (Ephesians 6:11).

Overhearing those children playing vampires was a wake-up call to me.

What legacy are we leaving the next generation?

What values have we instilled into their lives?

Do they understand there is a God who loves them?

Do they know they have a heavenly Father who sent His Son to die so that the Enemy of this world would be defeated?

My Own Personal Storm

When you find yourself in a spiritual battle, don't doubt in the dark what God has shown you in the light.[8] Sometimes the answer to God's dream for you comes through a storm. Keep your faith in the storms and know that God is orchestrating things behind the scenes.

Storms or trials can happen anywhere and at any time. No one knows when or where they will occur. They often come without warning.

On September 5, 2014, I was robbed. My purse was stolen out of my car in a shopping center parking lot in Johannesburg, South Africa. Yes, I locked the doors. However, we assume the thief used a gate remote or jamming device to prevent my doors from locking. I would normally take my purse with me, but I was only getting out of the car to ask a security guard for directions, so I chose to leave it under the driver's seat.

My purse contained my bank cards, passport, cell phone, university ID, digital camera, driver's license, calendar with personal information, and many other random things. They even stole the knob to my closet door that I was going to replace at the hardware store. In a split second, the world turned upside down, and I found myself in my own personal "storm."

The disciples of Jesus also found themselves in the middle of a storm:

> *That day when evening came, he said to his disciples, "Let us go over to the other side." Leaving the crowd behind, they took him along, just as he was, in the boat. There were also other boats with him. A furious squall came up, and the waves broke over the boat, so that it was nearly swamped. Jesus was in the stern, sleeping on a cushion. The disciples woke him and said to him, "Teacher, don't you care if we drown?"*
>
> *He got up, rebuked the wind and said to the waves, "Quiet! Be still!" Then the wind died down and it was completely calm.*

*He said to his disciples, "Why are you so afraid?
Do you still have no faith?" (Mark 4:35–40).*

When some people hear that I was robbed, they seem to assume that I did something wrong. In the Bible passage above, Jesus was the one who said that the ministry needed to move to the other side of the lake. It wasn't the disciples' decision—Jesus sent them into this storm.

Some storms are our fault. Other storms come because we obeyed the voice of God. Sometimes we question if we did the right thing. *Why didn't I just stay home that day? Why didn't I check my doors or take my purse with me?* But, if I had taken my purse with me, would they have attacked me instead? That very morning, my mother had felt prompted to pray that I wouldn't be raped. Could it be that God protected me from something even worse than theft?

The question is, "How do I respond to the storm?" Storms give us the opportunity to look to the One who brings peace to the storm. With my purse stolen, I didn't have money or a cell phone. The day after being robbed, I went to my South African bank to try to get a temporary card. They told me that without an ID they couldn't help me. They also brought up an issue from a few months before and stated that I shouldn't even have that bank account. In fact, as a foreigner, I was somehow illegal. In the midst of this, God's mercy prevailed, and I received a temporary card.

Then, at the cell phone store, the insurance company denied my claim to replace my stolen phone. I wrote them an email on Saturday, trusted in the Lord on Sunday, and on Monday the insurance claim was approved. Through these trials, God encouraged me that I can't overcome by my strength—only through His grace.

This storm did not blow over in a week or even a month. With my passport stolen, I had to apply for a new one. Every new passport has a new passport number. In South Africa, my passport number is my ID number. This meant that I needed to change my number on every account and document I had in South Africa. Also, my visa was in the passport, so a new one needed to be issued. With South African visa laws, this can prove very challenging and take a lot of time. My faith and trust had to remain in the Lord. If He'd called me to South Africa, then He would provide the means to live there.

You might ask God, "Why am I going through this storm?" Many times, God is just preparing our faith for something even greater. In Mark 5, there was a demoniac on the other side of the lake who needed deliverance. The storms teach us to walk by faith so that when we step out of the boat, we will be ready for the next experience. A greater challenge means a greater victory.

A greater challenge means a greater victory.

Is it any coincidence that my storm happened just as I was launching into a new ministry at the university? Or that on Friday I was robbed and on Tuesday the students started a strike on campus that turned violent? The truth is that I see now more than ever before that I'm in the middle of a spiritual battle. The Enemy does not want me on the university campuses of South Africa. He wants to discourage me and get me to quit. However, I won't quit, because I know that something even greater is awaiting me on the other side!

If you are in the middle of a storm, don't give up. God is preparing you for something even greater!

Here are some Scripture verses that encouraged me through this storm:

The God of peace will soon crush Satan under your feet (Romans 16:20a).

I consider that our present sufferings are not worth comparing with the glory that will be revealed in us (Romans 8:18).

And we know that in all things God works for the good of those who love him, who have been called according to his purpose (Romans 8:28).

If God is for us, who can be against us? (Romans 8:31b).

Who shall separate us from the love of Christ? Shall trouble or hardship or persecution or famine or nakedness or danger or sword? (Romans 8:35).

No, in all these things we are more than conquerors through him who loved us (Romans 8:37).

No weapon formed against you shall prosper (Isaiah 54:17a, NKJV).

"For my thoughts are not your thoughts, neither are your ways my ways," declares the Lord. "As the Heavens are higher than the earth, so are my ways higher than your ways and my thoughts than your thoughts" (Isaiah 55:8–9).

"Not by might nor by power, but by my Spirit," says the Lord Almighty. "What are you, O mighty mountain? . . . you will become level ground" (Zechariah 4:6b–7a).

The crime rate in South Africa was not the reason for my storm. I could have been robbed anywhere in the world. This trial was spiritual. The thief is not my enemy—the Devil is.

More Than I Can Handle

Many people say that "God will never give us more than we can handle." The truth is that sometimes the trial *is* more than we can handle. This is why we have to trust in the God who can calm the storm. The Bible says that He will never "tempt" us beyond what we can bear. This doesn't mean we won't have more "burdens" than we can carry (Matthew 11:28; Psalm 55:22).

> *No temptation has overtaken you except what is common to mankind. And God is faithful; he will not let you be tempted beyond what you can bear. But when you are tempted, he will also provide a way out so that you can endure it (1 Corinthians 10:13).*

God may test our faith through trials, but He will never lead us into any temptation that we cannot overcome (Luke 4:1–2, 13). A loving Father would never lead us to failure. He would never lead us to sin. He always provides a way to resist sin. God is holy. Sin separates us from God. Our Father desires that nothing would ever separate us from His love (Romans 8:38–39).

> *Consider it pure joy, my brothers and sisters, whenever you face trials of many kinds. . . . Blessed is the one who perseveres under trial because, having stood the test, that person will receive the crown of life that the Lord has promised to those who love him. When tempted, no one should say, "God is tempting me." For God cannot be tempted by evil, nor does he tempt anyone . . . (James 1:2, 12–13).*

God is not the source of our temptations. They come from Satan and our inner moral struggles. We must resist these ungodly desires. Satan uses temptations to provoke us into defying God. If we do not resist temptations, the result is spiritual "death" and separation from our Father.

We resist temptation, but we rejoice in our trials. Trials develop us into spiritually mature Christians.

Robbed Again

When I was robbed in 2014, it was very difficult for me to cope. Eventually, I found my way out of the darkness. Then, almost a year later, I was robbed again. This time it was my home.

I had picked up a mission team from the airport the day before. We had eaten dinner at a nearby mall. We Americans can sometimes be rather loud and draw attention to ourselves. I believe the robbers saw us at the mall and followed me home.

I was distracted by hosting the team, so I was not as observant as usual. I later remembered several people walking the streets near my house—many more than usual. The robbers probably watched our house that evening and waited for us to leave. When we finally left our home the next morning, they had their chance.

We went to do prayer walks on several campuses. A few minutes after we left, one of the campus leaders called and asked me to bring a printed email to reserve a venue on campus for our outreach. I had forgotten the paper in my office. I almost turned around to go home, but at the last minute, he said, "Don't worry about it. Just bring it tomorrow." If I had turned around, I probably would have encountered the robbers and faced real danger. God's protection was upon us.

At 12:20 p.m., my home alarm system went off. The alarm company can be rather slow, so it took 20 minutes for them to call me and say, "Ma'am, you have been robbed." The security guard had come to check the alarm and found the house broken into. However, the robbers were already long gone.

The mission team activities for the day were prayer walks and a youth service that evening. I quickly contacted the students who were going to pray with us to say that we would be unable to join them. Then I headed home.

When I arrived, I asked the team to remain in the car while I assessed the damage. My trusted gardener and a missionary friend were there waiting for me. Three security gates were broken. My security cameras had been moved so that the robbers would not be identified. As I walked into the house, I stepped over the door that now lay on the floor.

The robbers stole my television, ministry projector, brand new laptop, old laptop, and the mission team's laptop. I could tell that they had also gone through my jewelry, but there was nothing of value for them to steal.

After waiting three hours, the police finally came. As we filled out the police report for insurance, they sat at my dining room table sipping juice and enjoying conversation. The police officers admired my personal artwork displayed on the walls and went to get their iPad to take photos of it. When they left, I even gave one of the police officers a Bible.

That night we were supposed to share at the youth service in the Ga-Rankuwa township. I could have canceled, but I felt like I needed to persevere through the trial. I wasn't going to let the Devil win! While I took the team to the youth service, my gardener and one of the mission team leaders stayed behind to secure the door and gates.

As I hosted the team for the next few weeks, I decided to push forward and not let the robbery stop us from doing ministry. People called me to ask if I was okay. They wanted me to move to a different house with more security. They suggested I change security companies. Some even said I should sue the current company. Others said I needed to complain to the police. I put all of this aside and continued to focus on the work of the Kingdom.

This robbery was different from the first. I had been through this experience already and worked through some of the same feelings over the past year. This time I recognized that I was waging war with the Enemy. The ministry that the mission team did in those weeks took territory back from the Devil. He wasn't happy about what we were doing.

Trials often magnify other problems in our lives. I've learned to press through and not let the Devil win. Strongholds need to be broken, and we will feel the crossfire when we go into battle.

Some of the mission team members wrote me this letter as they said goodbye. They had seen the best and the worst of me. They witnessed me cry, laugh, and persevere.

> *Dear beautiful feet,*
>
> *Through the years we've learned that in ministry there are things that will go unseen. We manage to hear all about the triumphs in ministry, but seldom hear about all the battles and hardships on the road to triumph. These last few weeks have helped us understand the cost of following Christ a little better. Up until this point, we've realized how little we've sacrificed for the gospel. We've also learned how much emphasis we've put into pursuing the American Dream. . . .*

But as we worked with you we saw the love of Jesus radiating through you. You are the first person we have personally met that has given everything up for Jesus . . . so we thank you!

Thank you because we need more people like you in the world. More people who will go to the ends of the Earth to bring the hope of Jesus. More people who will leave their areas of comfort to make the name of Jesus known. We need more people who like you will say, "NO MATTER THE COST!"

So thank you, Sarah, for being a godly woman who pursues the things of Christ. And thank you for being transparent with us. It's nice to know you didn't sugar-coat things for us. . . . And even when you shed a tear or two we could see the strength of Jesus through you!

We admire you, Sarah, and we hope to meet again! We pray blessing over you, and we pray that the Lord would always bless you and keep you as you continue on this journey. Oh, beautiful feet . . . continue to change the world!

Love, Roxana & David

How, then, can they call on the one they have not believed in? And how can they believe in the one of whom they have not heard? And how can they hear without someone preaching to them? And how can anyone preach unless they are sent? As it is written: "How beautiful are the feet of those who bring good news!" (Romans 10:14–15).

Do you have beautiful feet? Are you bringing the good news of Jesus to others? Are you willing to accomplish God's dream—no matter the cost? Even if it means going to battle against the Enemy?

"The LORD will fight for you; you need only to be still" (Exodus 14:14).

"The Lord is your mighty defender, perfect and just in all his ways; Your God is faithful and true; he does what is right and fair" (Deuteronomy 32:4, GNT).

God is your Defender! He will be with you through every trial. He will fight for you. He will walk with you on the battlefield. He will give you peace to endure.

As you begin to step out in faith and fulfill God's dreams, you must recognize that you are indeed in a spiritual battle. When the trials come, don't despair. Rejoice that God is fighting for you! If you are facing difficulty, the Devil must be afraid. You have greatness in you. Otherwise, the Devil would just leave you alone. There is no need to fear because we know that we are on the winning team.

As you fulfill God's dream and the Enemy attacks, remember that God is your Defender.

CHAPTER EIGHT
WARTS AND JAWBONES (GOD, MY HEALER)

"Surely he took up our pain and bore our suffering, yet we considered him punished by God, stricken by him, and afflicted. But he was pierced for our transgressions, he was crushed for our iniquities; the punishment that brought us peace was on him, and by his wounds we are healed."
—Isaiah 53:4–5

God's dream is for us to be healed—physically, emotionally, and spiritually. The ultimate healing will take place in Heaven, but don't stop believing for healing to take place now. God calls us to walk in faith. He is a God of the impossible and the miraculous.

"Praise the Lord, O my soul, and forget not all his benefits—who forgives all your sins and heals all your diseases" (Psalm 103:2–3). God's dream is to heal all our diseases. When Jesus died on the cross, He not only took our sins upon Himself but "by his wounds we are healed." He did not say that we *might* be healed or *could* be healed. He said we *are* healed.

God wants to heal you. He is the same yesterday, today, and forever (Hebrews 13:8). If He healed in the Bible, He will heal today. He doesn't have favorites (Romans 2:11). He wants *all* to be healed. Sickness is Satan's work (Job 2:7). Jesus came to destroy the work of Satan (1 John 3:8).

Warts

When I was in the first grade, I had a wart on my elbow. Kids were cruel and would often make fun of me. I was so short that I sat in a booster seat in our family car. The cracked plastic armrest would cut my wart and even tear it off. This pain and the humiliation at school was too much.

One Sunday at church, I asked my mom if she would pray with me at the altar. We prayed for God to take my wart away. The wart did not fall off at that very moment, but within a week it slowly disappeared. To this day, I'm wart free.

If God cared about my wart, how much more does he care about all our needs? He was responding to my childlike faith and affirming that God is able! "For with God nothing will be impossible" (Luke 1:37, NKJV).

Jesus wants us to ask for our healing in faith. He promises to do anything we need when we ask him (John 14:13–14).

> *Is anyone among you sick? Let them call the elders of the church to pray over them and anoint them with oil in the name of the Lord. And the prayer offered in*

faith will make the sick person well; the Lord will raise them up. If they have sinned, they will be forgiven. Therefore confess your sins to each other and pray for each other so that you may be healed. The prayer of a righteous person is powerful and effective (James 5:14–16).

In the American church, I grew up anointing the sick with oil. In the African church, the use of oil can be abused or associated with some of the rituals people performed before being born again. People even put faith in the oil instead of the God who heals them.

Our faith is not in the oil—our faith is in the God who heals! Your prayers are powerful and effective. You don't need any anointed object. You don't need to go to Nigeria or Jerusalem for your healing. The prayer of faith brings the healing.

All you need is faith. It is God's will to heal you, simply by the prayer offered in faith! "This is the confidence we have in approaching God: that if we ask anything according to his will, he hears us. And if we know that he hears us—whatever we ask—we know that we have what we asked of him" (1 John 5:14–15).

When you pray for healing, you can have confidence that you are asking for God's will for your life. God hears your

When you pray for healing, you can have confidence that you are asking for God's will for your life.

prayers! You must walk in faith even when you don't see the answer yet. "Now faith is confidence in what we hope for and assurance about what we do not see" (Hebrews 11:1).

God honors faith.

In South Africa, many false teachers promise miracles. They have tried to deceive people into believing in their miraculous signs. However, just because there is a "miracle" doesn't mean it was from God. The power of Satan can also replicate some miracles. Exodus 7:22 says that "the Egyptian magicians did the same things by their secret arts. . . ."

Though some people have tried to heal falsely, that doesn't mean we should not believe that healing is real. In fact, some real healings have taken place at churches led by false teachers. I believe that is because of the faith of the individual.

> *It is true that some preach Christ out of envy and rivalry, but others out of goodwill. The latter do so out of love, knowing that I am put here for the defense of the gospel. The former preach Christ out of selfish ambition, not sincerely, supposing that they can stir up trouble for me while I am in chains. But what does it matter? The important thing is that in every way, whether from false motives or true, Christ is preached. And because of this I rejoice. Yes, and I will continue to rejoice . . . (Philippians 1:15–18).*

If someone has faith to be healed, God will heal them. It doesn't matter if the pastor was walking in the truth or not. God has compassion on the person and honors their faith in any situation. What matters is that they are healed!

Whether it's a wart or any other sickness, God cares.

Why?

If God cares so much, then why does He allow sickness? Why would He allow the righteous to suffer?

"'Neither this man nor his parents sinned,' said Jesus, 'but this happened so that the works of God might be displayed in him'" (John 9:3).

Some people want to blame God, the Devil, their parents, or sin for sickness. However, sometimes there is no cause other than our fallen world. Sickness is part of the curse (Deuteronomy 28:15, 21–22, 58–61) that Jesus came to set us free from (Galatians 3:13). God does not cause sickness, but He may allow sickness in our lives. God's dream is that His healing power will be revealed in our lives.

How can there still be someone in a wheelchair? Couldn't God heal them? Is it because of their lack of faith? Sometimes it is a lack of faith, but at other times we have to trust in God's timing and dream for our lives.

I believe that it is God's will to heal all of us. We should never give up believing for healing. However, the real question is this: "How can the works of God be displayed in your life?" Sometimes God allows us to experience suffering so that others can see the work of Jesus in us.

Jesus died on a cross. He suffered the ultimate pain and death so that we could have a relationship with Him. Why should we not be willing to suffer so that others can come to faith? Jesus knew the suffering would not end in death; after three days He would rise again. We know that the same power that raised Jesus from the dead lives in us.

"And if the Spirit of him who raised Jesus from the dead is living in you, he who raised Christ from the dead will also give life to your mortal bodies because of his Spirit who lives in you" (Romans 8:11).

The Spirit gives life to our mortal bodies! It doesn't say "heavenly" bodies. We don't have to wait for Heaven to be healed. The Holy Spirit lives in us! Have faith that God can heal you now. Pray for God to be glorified through your healing.

The Dancing Granny

During my first six months in South Africa, I traveled to a village with Wayne and Delight Peercy. A 17-year-old boy had committed suicide, so we went to console the family. When we arrived at the small mud hut, we parked our car in the only available place—under the shade tree in which the young man had hanged himself.

The family told us that when they had found him hanging in the tree, they left his body until the police came. The police also left him hanging there for some time. People had started coming to look and talk. The grandmother was very upset by it all.

After the funeral, they served juice and biscuits. We were then invited to pray for the family.

There was another grandmother in the mud hut. She sat on a mat on the dirt floor. The boy who'd died had cared for her and carried her wherever she needed to go. She was distraught over his death. As we prayed for the family, she asked that we also pray for her legs because she had not walked in three years.

The local pastor, Wayne, Delight, and I all laid hands on the granny as we prayed the prayer of faith. As we said, "Amen," I was ready to walk out the door. However, Delight quickly said, "Let's help her to her feet and see if she can walk."

This shocked me. I was guilty of not really believing, just going through the motions of "church." How many times do we pray and not even check to see if God answered our prayers? Do we genuinely believe?

> How many times do we pray and not even check to see if God answered our prayers?

We helped the granny up off the dirt floor. She began moving her feet and soon started to dance. Her family started crying from joy and praising God. You could tell by their reaction that this granny was moving in a way she had not in a very long time. God had healed her!

After this, we all sang and danced. Tears of joy fell from my eyes. Our mourning had turned to dancing.

What if we had only prayed and not checked to see if God had answered? Our faith often needs to be followed by action. Many times in the Bible, people were healed as they acted in faith. One example is the story of Jesus healing the 10 lepers.

"When he saw them, he said, 'Go, show yourselves to the priests.' And as they went, they were cleansed" (Luke 17:14). The lepers were healed as they went. The lepers would have to be declared clean by the priests to return to normal society. They didn't wait until they saw their healing. They believed they were cleansed, and as they went, they were!

The sad part of my story of the dancing granny is the young boy who committed suicide. He ended his life without hope for the future. "'For I know the plans I have for you,' declares the Lord, 'plans to prosper you and not to harm you, plans to give you hope and a future'" (Jeremiah 29:11).

God's dream is always to give us hope and a future. It's never His will for anyone to take their own life. I don't know what that young man was going through. Maybe he was mentally, emotionally, or spiritually sick. But no matter what kind of healing we seek, we can believe that there is hope. Let's trust that Jesus is our Healer, and never give up.

When God is Silent

Do you sometimes feel that God is silent? I do. In the book *My Utmost for His Highest,* Oswald Chambers describes how hard it must have been for Mary and Martha in the days of silence after their brother Lazarus' death. It seemed like Jesus had forgotten them and didn't care. They had no cell phones to find out where He was. There was only silence.

"When He heard that he was sick, He stayed two more days in the place where He was" (John 11:6). Jesus didn't rush to heal Lazarus. He waited. However, Jesus' silence paved the way for a greater miracle. Instead of healing Lazarus' illness, Jesus raised him from the dead! Chambers said, "God's silences are actually His answers."

Has God trusted you with a silent moment?

Time is nothing to God. We must trust Him through the silence. Though I don't know all the answers, I'm thankful for the reassurance of God's presence.

When God doesn't heal right away, we need to trust that He's delaying the healing to show His glory—just like Lazarus' sickness wasn't cured so that there would be a greater miracle.

How can your healing journey be used to save others?

Do you feel like your faith is not great enough? God only asks for a small amount of faith. He helps us overcome our unbelief. He calls us not to give up.

"If you have faith as small as a mustard seed, you can say to this mulberry tree, 'Be uprooted and planted in the sea,' and it will obey you" (Luke 17:6).

"Immediately the boy's father exclaimed, 'I do believe; help me overcome my unbelief!'" (Mark 9:24).

Do you just want to give up? God always calls us to persevere. Like the persistent widow, we should keep praying until He answers our request. Don't stop believing that the healing can take place now—not just in Heaven.

Then Jesus told his disciples a parable to show them that they should always pray and not give up. He said: "In a certain town there was a judge who neither feared God nor cared what people thought. And there was a widow in that town who kept coming to him with the plea, 'Grant me justice against my adversary.'

"For some time he refused. But finally he said to himself, 'Even though I don't fear God or care what people think, yet because this widow keeps bothering me, I will see that she gets justice, so that she won't eventually come and attack me!'"

And the Lord said, "Listen to what the unjust judge says. And will not God bring about justice for his chosen ones, who cry out to him day and night? Will he keep putting them off? I tell you, he will see that they get justice, and quickly. However, when the Son of Man comes, will he find faith on the earth?" (Luke 18:1–8).

If an unjust judge will hear the cries of a widow, how much more will God bring justice to His chosen ones? Let's believe the Word of God and not doubt that He does desire our healing. Let's pray the prayer of faith, even if it's only the size of a mustard seed.

Jawbones

Like any good parent, my mom took me to the dentist for check-ups. When I was in the sixth grade, our dentist told my parents that I had a severe underbite. My bottom teeth were in front of my top teeth, and there was a gap between them. When I bit into a sandwich, the lunchmeat always slid out. One positive thing about my underbite was that I never got into the habit of biting my fingernails; it was impossible.

The dentist suggested that we try to fix my underbite with braces. I wore braces for over a year, but they were unable to correct my jaw. The only way to fix it would be surgery. My jaw would have to be broken and screwed back together. This procedure was extremely expensive. In fact, the cost was nearly equal to my parents' annual salary. The cost and fear of pain helped us decide just to live with it and not do surgery. God created me and formed me in my mother's womb. Surely, I could live with my "deformity."

However, my childlike faith never gave up. Many times at church, I would pray at the altar for healing. When the service ended, I would run to look in the church bathroom mirror to see if God had healed me.

When I was in high school, one of my front teeth went so crooked that I got braces again. The retainer came loose, and the tooth went crooked again, so I got braces for the third time. The next retainer was different, but again, my teeth moved. By this time I was tired of it all! I had the dentist artificially make my teeth look straight and cement a retainer to the backs of my teeth in hopes that they would never move again.

Years later, I shared this story with one of my African friends. Africans have great faith (remember the African granny who regained strength in her legs and danced for the Lord?). My friend's comments made me feel like my faith was not strong enough for God to heal me. This frustrated me. I did have faith.

God hears our prayers. He is the Healer. But sometimes He answers, "Not yet." Not every answer to prayer is a sudden miracle. Some miracles come later, and some even come through doctors. Sometimes our healing will only be seen in Heaven. God loves me and cares about my infirmities. But I've come to realize that my life's purpose is not about me. My life is about bringing glory to God. What if our sicknesses or deformities bring more glory to God than our healing?

20 years after being told that I needed jaw surgery, I went to a South African dentist for a cleaning. My American dentist had stopped commenting on the fact that I needed the surgery. I guess they gave up on me. Now the South African dentist told me that I needed to have jaw surgery. Then a few months later, my retainer felt like it had come loose, so I went to a South African orthodontist. He also told me that I should seriously think about having this surgery.

My childhood nightmare had resurfaced. I thought I had put all of this behind me. By now, you must realize how much I despised going to the dentist and orthodontist. In America, my dentist would sometimes use me as his "guinea pig" to show all the new dental hygienists what an extreme underbite looked like. This made me feel ugly and deformed—like I was abnormal.

Then I realized that maybe this was not another nightmare. Perhaps God was answering my childhood prayers! After doing some research, I found out that the surgery in South Africa was not as expensive as it had been when I was a child in America. I thought it might be possible with my savings. In fact, the more I thought about the cost, I realized that the amount of money I had just spent on two couches and curtains for my new home could pay for the orthodontics and surgery. My healing was worth more than two couches!

TMJ (temporomandibular joint disorder) was a problem that I suffered with because of my jaw. As missionaries, we have to preach often and talk with people before and after each church service. There were some Sundays when I felt like I had an ear infection.

After going to the doctor, he explained that it wasn't my ear hurting but my jaw. He actually said, "This is common among women because they talk too much." (Seriously! Like women talk too much.)

In February 2016, I got braces for the fourth time in my life. (Hopefully, the last!) That November, the oral surgeon operated on my jaw. For the first week after the surgery, I could only drink liquids. In the second and the third week, I could only have soft foods. My face was swollen and bruised. I had sleepless nights and side effects from the pain medication.

For over a month after the surgery, the right side of my chin remained numb. I couldn't feel my face. If I dribbled soup down my chin, family members and friends had to let me know to wipe off my face. I felt like a baby while eating.

Gradually, I could eat more, the swelling and bruising faded, and the extreme numbness went away.

A few months after the surgery, my braces came off, and I could smile again. In fact, I could now bite properly! I am thankful for the doctors, but I give God the glory!

God orchestrated events for me to have the procedure done in South Africa. In fact, He even touched the heart of a supporter to help cover the cost. God provided the surgery and the finances for it!

Sometimes our healing comes miraculously, and other times, God uses a doctor. In my case, this surgery is a testimony that God heard my childhood prayers. He did heal me!

Empowered to Heal

God dreams that you would not just believe in healing for your own life but that you would also pray for the healing of others. As we minister to the lost and disciple believers, we should pray for their healing. God promises that He will heal. We can do even greater things than Jesus did.

> God dreams that you would not just believe in healing for your own life but that you would also pray for the healing of others.

"Very truly I tell you, whoever believes in me will do the works I have been doing, and they will do even greater things than these, because I am going to the Father" (John 14:12).

"And these signs will accompany those who believe . . . they will place their hands on sick people and they will get well" (Mark 16:17a–18b).

When you pray for others, will you pray the prayer of faith over them?

The Holy Spirit is in us, and we have the capacity to see people healed. Many times our lack of faith will extinguish what God can do, but we should not allow the possibility of doubt to stop us from praying.

Sometimes I've been afraid to pray for the sick. What if God doesn't heal them? I've realized that God can defend Himself. He can defend His character. My job is to pray in faith and believe that God can heal the person. Then I need to leave the outcome in God's hand. The moment I say, "God, if it be your will," I have put doubt in our hearts. It is God's will to heal!

God is calling you to increase your faith. Believe that God wants to heal you. He wants to heal your loved ones. He also wants you to pray for others, even strangers, to be healed.

God can use doctors. He can also perform miracles. Though we may go to a doctor, we should never lose faith that God can do the miracle.

In Africa, many people cannot afford to go to the doctor. I believe this is why we see more miraculous healings here. The people are required to have faith in God because they have no other option. They can't trust in the doctor. They must trust in their God.

Healing isn't just for our physical bodies. God also wants to heal us spiritually, mentally, and emotionally. God's dream is that you would be the vessel to bring that healing to others.

Jesus declared that God had anointed Him for the ministry. I believe He is calling us to walk in the same anointing of the Spirit. Will you speak these verses out loud over your life, just as Jesus did?

> *The Spirit of the Lord is on me,*
> *because he has anointed me*
> *to proclaim good news to the poor.*
> *He has sent me to proclaim freedom for the prisoners*
> *and recovery of sight for the blind,*
> *to set the oppressed free,*
> *to proclaim the year of the Lord's favor*
> *(Luke 4:18–19).*

(Did you really say them out loud? If not, go ahead and do it.)

God has anointed you to accomplish His dream to bring healing to others. When you walk in faith, you will bring physical and spiritual healing to others. Don't limit what God wants to do in and through your life.

Will you introduce others to the God who heals?

PART THREE
SURRENDER YOUR DREAM

CHAPTER NINE
NEVER ALONE (DREAM TEAMS)

"Now you are the body of Christ, and each one of you is a part of it."
—1 Corinthians 12:27

God's dream is not *my* dream. It is *our* dream. Only the body of Christ can accomplish the enormous task before us. Everyone has a part to play.

Even Jesus worked with a team of disciples. Elijah had Elisha, Moses had Joshua, Barnabas had Paul, and Paul had Timothy. Sometimes there may be a conflict between team members, as when Paul was upset that Mark deserted him on their missionary journey (Acts 13:13; 15:38). However, Paul later asked for Mark to join the team again because he would be useful (2 Timothy

4:11). As the body of Christ, we have to embrace our differences. Teamwork makes the dream work!

> *Then he said to his disciples, "The harvest is plentiful but the workers are few. Ask the Lord of the harvest, therefore, to send out workers into his harvest field" (Matthew 9:37–38).*

I've battled loneliness on the mission field. I've prayed that God would send laborers to help with the work and be companions for me. At times the task is overwhelming; the needs seem endless.

One of the greatest examples of teamwork is marriage. God created us to work as a team. In the book of Genesis, God said, "It is not good for man to be alone" (Genesis 2:18). God created a suitable helper for Adam: his wife, Eve. In a marriage, each partner shares responsibility and cooperates to fulfill God's dream for their lives. Marriage is a picture of Jesus' partnership with the church.

If you are single, don't worry. There is still a team for you. You don't need a spouse to have a partnership. Just as Jesus surrounded Himself with disciples, we should surround ourselves with a team. The body of Christ is made up of many parts. We must learn to embrace others' differences and build upon our weaknesses with their strengths.

In God's Kingdom, we are better together than alone.

Has Someone Failed God?

Victor Plymire was a missionary to Tibet. His wife and son died on the mission field. After their deaths, he wrote this in a letter:

On January 29, I followed my two loved ones to this lonely spot on the Tibetan mountains. My dear wife and little boy were placed in one grave. Why these dear ones were called away I do not know. I do not question. They were so earnest in trying to evangelize this vast region. It is very hard in the natural, now entirely alone. We begged for someone to come help my wife in the work and to be a companion while I was out among the Tibetans. But no one came. Has someone failed God?[9]

There have been times when I've prayed for help and no one came. Did someone fail God?

At the same time, I was never alone! God was part of my team.

There have been other times when God answered my prayers for co-laborers in the harvest field. In 2010 and 2011, Jessica White (now Jessica Wilson) joined my team as we developed the National Youth Ministries in South Africa. I would never have completed the work without her help.

There have been times when I've prayed for help and no one came. Did someone fail God?

To be honest, when I was without a co-laborer, I struggled with jealousy of other "dream teams." In the state of Indiana, university ministry has exploded. Praise God! Currently, there are campus ministries at almost every major university in Indiana. Each campus has a full-time pastor with volunteer staff and student leaders. In South Africa, at times I was the only ministry leader for many campuses. It didn't seem fair to me. Where was my dream team?

While I was home in 2015 for my brother's wedding, I attended a pastors' meeting along with several of those

US-based university missionaries. The weight of the ministry needs in South Africa weighed so heavily on me that I asked several of those serving on campuses in America if they would be willing to come to South Africa. No one felt "called" to help me. My heart broke.

The following year, God provided Samantha Hanson to help me. God had called her to leave her comfort zone in Minnesota and serve in South Africa. She helped teach the weekly Bible studies at the universities and developed our student leaders so that they could plant small groups and missional communities. The impact she made in those students' lives will last for eternity.

When I had team members, there were moments I was guilty of focusing on how they could help me rather than how I could help them. I acted as if they were sent to serve me—not the other way around. God had to correct this attitude. As a missionary, God has called me to mentor others to be the future missionaries of the world. My dream team needs to go beyond myself.

Jealousy also emerged when I compared myself to my co-laborers. Were they better at ministry than me? Why did it seem that everyone loved them more than me? Eventually, I had to embrace who God made me to be. I am not them. They are not me. God made us all individuals with unique talents and gifts. Each of us should be who God created us to be. We are called to rejoice in the success of our teammates. Their victories are wins for the team.

God's dream team is made up of many parts. Though we may be gifted more in one area than another, everyone is called to pray, give, and go. The real question is will we obey? Will we work together to make God's dreams come true? Or is the body of Christ sick because part of the team is not participating?

The Sending Team

My work would not be possible without those who partnered to send me. These individuals are praying and sacrificing to support the mission financially. The work they make possible is credited to their heavenly reward. They are a vital part of the team.

Prayer Partners

Never underestimate the power of prayer. It is the reason the Enemy's plans have been demolished here in South Africa, and it's why I have so much favor with God.

God's dream team includes the body of Christ joining in prayer for one another.

> *I thank my God every time I remember you. In all my prayers for all of you, I always pray with joy because of your partnership in the gospel from the first day until now, being confident of this, that he who began a good work in you will carry it on to completion until the day of Christ Jesus (Philippians 1:3–6).*

Paul prayed for the Philippian church with joy and confidence that God would complete the work He began. We should also pray for one another with bold prayers of faith.

One church in Michigan regularly sends me emails asking about my prayer needs. Their communication helps me know that I am not alone, and their prayers are with me.

Every time I send out a newsletter update on the mission work, I include prayer requests—not because it helps fill space on a page, but because I believe in the power of prayer. As the body of Christ unites over specific needs, Heaven listens.

Prayer changes things.

Financial Partners

God's dream team also includes those who give financially to the work. Ministry requires money. God honors the sacrifice of those who give. It's not about the quantity but the sacrifice.

The apostle Paul would not have been able to survive on his missionary journeys if it were not for the generosity of the Philippian church.

> *Moreover, as you Philippians know, in the early days of your acquaintance with the gospel, when I set out from Macedonia, not one church shared with me in the matter of giving and receiving, except you only; for even when I was in Thessalonica, you sent me aid again and again when I was in need (Philippians 4:15–16).*

God's dream team includes those who give financially.

Short-Term Mission Teams

You may not live as a full-time missionary in a foreign country, but that doesn't mean that you can never "go" (Matthew 28:19–20). Many teams come here for a few weeks to serve alongside a missionary. More can be accomplished when we work together.

Short-term teams have helped us reach the universities in South Africa. Every time a team comes, I've been able to evangelize the university campuses like never before. We often host movie nights with the extra help from the team. Hundreds of students come to hear the gospel message.

I've heard stories of how team members complained throughout a mission trip and only wanted a glorified vacation to tell their friends about. They wouldn't eat the food and refused to do certain kinds of ministry. This has not been the case for the teams I've hosted, but I share this to say *dream beyond yourself*! For a few weeks, do something that's not about your comfort. Be willing to embrace something different than what you've always known so that someone might be introduced to a God they've never known.

Going on a short-term trip may change your life more than the nationals' as God's dream begins to sink deep into your heart.

The Missionary Team

Deciding to give up your family and all that you've known for the long term is not an easy decision. But it usually takes a great sacrifice to make a great impact.

Some people will never listen to you talk about the God you serve until you have lived among them and proven your love for them. This cannot be accomplished in a week. It may take months, years—even decades.

Each missionary has different gifts and talents (1 Corinthians 12:27). Some work with children, others teach at Bible Schools, some are providing clean water solutions, and others build tabernacles or plant churches. I work with youth, young adults, and university students. We all have different abilities, but we work together to equip the national church and reach lost people.

We are a team that becomes a family.

When I left my family in the USA, God provided another family for me: the missionaries and nationals.

Sometimes my church family and missionary family feel even closer to me than some of my biological family.

On the mission field, the missionary children call other missionaries "Aunt" and "Uncle." We spend holidays together, laugh and cry together, and work together to accomplish the mission.

Some Africans have become my closest friends in the past 10 years. We celebrate birthdays with cake and a day of adventure. We cry over the death of a friend and rejoice at weddings. My African family often introduces me as a daughter, sister, or mother.

Though I have sacrificed precious memories with my birth family and I cherish the moments I spend with them, I am also grateful for God's provision of the family of God—no matter where I am in the world.

The National Team

In South Africa, I have the national people on my team. Who is wiser and better qualified to reach South Africans than other South Africans?

The national people are our most significant team members. They are the ones who will keep the work going and see God's dreams fulfilled for their land.

For the most part, the days when a "white" person or missionary came into a country and ran the church are gone. This is because many countries have developed a national church, so the missionary must work in partnership with local church leaders. In other countries, where people are still unreached, the missionary may need to establish a church. However, no matter the situation, a partnership with the national people is vital.

As a missionary, I believe I have learned more from my African brothers and sisters than they have learned from me. My work in South Africa has been successful because of the team God placed around me.

One of those team members is Dr. Gordon Lebelo who serves as a local pastor and the General President of the International Assemblies of God (IAG) church. When I arrived in South Africa in 2009, he was also the National Youth Director. My assignment was to help develop the National Youth Ministries for the IAG.

I thought my experience in youth ministry was limited. I had never held the title of youth pastor; I had only assisted a youth pastor. I felt that I was the least qualified person for the job. But God guided me through Dr. Lebelo's wisdom. His dreams became my dreams. I made it my goal to make his dreams come true for the youth of the IAG. Because I embraced the national church's vision, the ministry was a success.

The National Youth Ministries now has more team members. There is a National Youth Director with seven youth committee members on the national team. The national church currently has 11 districts with district youth committees who work with the local church's youth committees. All of these leaders are part of God's dream team. Everyone has a different role. If they all work together, the youth of Africa will be saved.

Holy Spirit Partnership

One of the blessings God gave me in South Africa was the friendship of Grace. Grace is a South African about the same age as me. When I first came to South Africa, she was living with the Peercy family, and she became my roommate. Grace explained to me the African way of doing things and even taught me how to dance. Living with her gave me a perspective on African culture that many other missionaries are not able to have.

One of the songs Grace taught me says "If you believe and I believe, and we together pray, The Holy Spirit must come down, and Africa will be saved." This song reminds me that we all need to work together for Africa to be saved. This partnership is threefold: The missionary and the national people work together with the Holy Spirit.

The Holy Spirit is the central member of the team (Acts 1:8). Without Him, we will never move forward. If you ever feel alone, remember that Jesus promised that the Holy Spirit would be with you "always, to the very end of the age" (Matthew 28:20).

The life of the church is in the hands of the national people. They will stay and carry on the work long after the missionary is gone. With the power of the Holy Spirit, the church can grow and develop to the point where they also send missionaries to unreached areas. They will no longer only receive but also give to impact this world for Jesus.

The Unfinished Task

The gospel must be preached to the whole world, and then Christ will return (Matthew 24:14). Why then has it not been done?

Yes, the enemy is fighting against it, and there are some closed doors. But one of the major problems is the matter of laborers. In the past, missionaries often went alone. Now, many unreached places require a team of workers. Some of the closed doors are opening, but there are not enough laborers ready to go through.

Will you pray with me for the missionary team? As you pray, would you ask God if you are meant to be part of the team?

Do we understand that people are lost without Jesus? Some say that if people are not lost until they hear, why even do missions? If only those who reject Christ will go to Hell, we should never tell anyone about Him, right?[10] This is a lie from the Enemy. "Salvation is found in no one else, for there is no other name under heaven given to men by which we must be saved" (Acts 4:12).

Do we understand that people are lost without Jesus?

"Jesus answered, 'I am the way and the truth and the life. No one comes to the Father except through me'" (John 14:6). Islam, Buddhism, Hinduism, and all other religions will not save someone from an eternity in Hell. Only Jesus can save them!

Since becoming a missionary, I've realized the great need for more people to spread the gospel. There are still people who have never heard of Jesus. They have never had the opportunity to choose salvation. They are known as UPGs (Unreached People Groups).

According to the Joshua Project, the world has 16,825 people groups. 6,989 of these are still unreached. The population of today's world is 7.47 billion people. 42.2% of the world's population remains unreached.[11]

There are also reached places that still need our partnership. Many missionaries are getting old and are about to retire. God needs to raise up the next generation to carry on their work.

The world must be evangelized. Why not complete this task in our generation?[12]

The Assemblies of God university movement has asked students to "give a year and pray about a lifetime" of serving in missions. My prayer is for the next generation to give at least one year of their lives on the mission field and pray about giving a lifetime. Let's dream beyond ourselves and answer God's call to reach the lost.

God has called everyone to *go*. We must obey and listen to His voice to learn *where* He has called us.

How can you know if you are called for the long term if you've never gone at all?

Are you the team member others are praying for?

There is No "I" in Team

God's dream team should be one that walks in unity.

When we hear the word *unity*, we tend to focus on the opposite: disunity. We think about divisions in local churches and how this person can't get along with that person. We try to fix those broken relationships to achieve unity.

However, true unity between believers is a reflection of their relationship with God. If we are right "vertically" with God, then we will be right "horizontally" in our relationships with people. In the body of Christ, we are told that Jesus is the head (Colossian 1:18). If we all make sure we are connected to Jesus, then we will be unified in working together for Christ's purposes.

> *I pray that out of his glorious riches he may strengthen you with power through his Spirit in your inner being, so that Christ may **dwell** in your hearts through faith. And I pray that you, **being rooted and established in love**, may have **power**, together with all the saints to **grasp how wide and long and high and deep is the love of Christ**, and to know this love that surpasses knowledge—that you may be filled to the measure of all the fullness of God. **Now to him who is able to do immeasurably more that all we ask or imagine, according to his power that is at work within us,***

to him be glory in the church and in Christ Jesus throughout all generations, forever and ever! Amen.

As a prisoner for the Lord, then, I urge you **to live a life worthy of the calling** *you have received. Be completely humble and gentle; be patient, bearing with one another in love.* **Make every effort to keep the unity** *of the Spirit through the bond of peace (Ephesians 3:16–4:3, emphasis added).*

There is "Love" in Team

To maintain unity, we must first be rooted and established in love.

"Being rooted" in God's love is like a plant digging deep roots into the soil. "Being established" in His love is like a building having a strong foundation laid on solid rock.

Both metaphors symbolize depth in our relationship with God. The revelation of the love of Christ is necessary for us to have a deep, solid relationship with Him. You must "grasp how wide and long and high and deep is the love of Christ . . . that you may be filled to the measure of all the fullness of God"!

If we are born again and in love with Jesus, how can we not love our brothers and keep the unity (1 John 4:7–12, 19–21)? Loving others is not about trying harder. It's about desiring God more.

Dream teams are about loving people. If we do not love people, we do not love God.

What we do to help God's people in need actually helps the Lord Himself (Matthew 25:40). When we love people, we help accomplish God's dream.

If you are going to be on a team, you have to love the people on the team. God's dream teams are not about holding a position or title. This isn't a 9-to-5 job. You can't just do the work and go home. God's dream team involves loving every team member with "the affection of Christ Jesus" (Philippians 1:8). It's about loving beyond yourself.

There is "Power" in Team

To keep the unity, we must be connected to the power source: the Holy Spirit. Everyone wants to quote "God will do immeasurably more than all we can ask or imagine." However, the verse is conditional: "according to his power that is at work within us."

The branch must connect to the vine (John 15:7).

The body must connect to the head (Colossians 1:18).

For us not to walk in the flesh, the Holy Spirit must fill us (Galatians 5:13–16).

Let's live by the Spirit, be filled with the Holy Spirit, and allow God's power to work in us and through us.

There is "Calling" in Team

To live in unity, we must be dedicated to living worthy of the calling. So what is your calling? What is God's dream for your life?

Jesus says in John 17:20–21, ". . . I pray also for those who will believe in me through their message, that all of them may be one, Father, just as you are in me and I am in you. May they also be in us so that the world may believe that you have sent me."

The main reason for unity in *God's team* is so people will know that Jesus was sent by the Father to bring them back into a relationship with God—"that they may believe that you have sent me." Christ's followers will not be effective in leading others to Him unless they are living in unity. Without unity, their testimony lacks credibility.

When outside forces threaten to divide God's dream team, remember that Paul says our struggle is not against other people but Satan (Ephesians 6:12).

Maybe you are experiencing disunity with a person or group. Take a moment to recommit to being rooted in love, staying connected to the power source, and living a life worthy of your calling. If you have a grievance against someone, I encourage you to forgive.

If you want to be successful on God's dream team, you have to love people. Look beyond their differences and embrace who God has called them to be. All of our lives will be woven together into a beautiful tapestry to accomplish God's great dream of reaching this world.

Inside the Riverbanks

As a missionary, I have to be careful not to come into a country with my own plans. It's not about *my* dream but *our* dream, which is ultimately *God's* dream. Every missionary should work toward the same vision and goal: build the national church.

This vision is the river that moves the team forward. If any team member moves outside of the vision, they may slow down the progress of the team. Floodwaters outside the riverbanks invite disaster.

What is the vision that moves your team forward? Does your dream fit into God's dream? The river is moving in one direction. Are you inside the riverbanks of what God is doing, or have you drifted outside with your own dream and plan?

When working in a team, there is usually an

experienced team leader. We must be willing to work together and submit to our leader's guidance.

An old African proverb says, "If you want to go fast, go alone. If you want to go far, go together."

How can we work together to go far in the same direction?

We have to ask ourselves, "What's best for the greater vision of the church and the world?" Will you surrender *your* dream for *our* dream?

What team is God asking you to be a part of?

Is someone waiting for you to fill the missing spot on their team?

Will they ask "Has someone failed God?" or will you answer the call?

CHAPTER TEN

TRUE LOVE WAITED . . . AND WAITED . . . AND WAITED. . . . (DREAMS UNFULFILLED)

"So do not throw away your confidence; it will be richly rewarded. You need to persevere so that when you have done the will of God, you will receive what he has promised."
—Hebrews 10:35–36

What happens when you have a dream and feel that it is from God, yet it remains unfulfilled? God calls us to trust in His plan and wait on Him. While we wait, we must spend our time serving Him. We must choose not to dwell on the dream of what might be, but instead, choose to rejoice in every day the Lord has made.

Hannah dreamed of having a child, but she was barren. Peninnah, her rival, continually provoked her (1

Samuel 1:6). This went on for years. Eventually, Hannah went to the house of the Lord and prayed for her dream.

At first, Eli the priest thought she was drunk, but he soon recognized that this woman was desperately crying out to God. He encouraged her that God would grant her request. Before the dream was fulfilled, Hannah got up from the altar rejoicing that God had heard her prayer (1 Samuel 1:1–20).

Like Hannah, we should get up from the altar and rejoice that God has heard our prayer. At God's appointed time, the dream will be realized.

True Love Waits

In my life, the unfulfilled dream that has been the hardest to keep trusting God for is for a spouse. I've always wanted to marry and have my own family. I thought this would have happened years ago; but for some reason, it has been delayed until God's appointed time.

Most girls dream of their wedding day. *You are walking down the aisle in a beautiful white dress and look into his eyes*—but whose eyes are they? Have I already met the guy? Will I meet him this year or in five years? How long am I going to have to wait?

Proverbs 18:22 says, "He who finds a wife finds what is good and receives favor from the LORD." After reading this Scripture, I would cry, "Lord, I'm waiting to be found!" All the guys probably ask God, "Lord, where is she? How do I find her?"

As a teenager, I went to purity events like the "True Love Waits" rally. My parents even gave me a purity ring to wear until my wedding day. But there came a point when I became tired of "waiting." I'm not talking about purity here—I am waiting to have sex only in marriage. What I'm saying is that I wasn't going to wait to live my life. I was going to live to the fullest for God with or without a spouse.

There have been times when I've wondered, "Is something wrong with me? Why am I still not married? Am I ugly?" However, I now realize that these are lies from the Enemy to discourage me. I am a beautiful creation of the Lord! And so are you!

I've never dated. I've never kissed a boy. There have only been a few times when a potential guy seemed interested. Because I felt they were not the one for me, I kindly gave them the hint that I wasn't interested. Then I would question, "Did I push the right guy away? Is that why I'm still single?" But I believe I've learned to hear the leading of the Holy Spirit, so I don't think I've missed God's plan.

God has kept me in His hands through the years, and I've remained pure. God has used my purity to inspire other young people so that they will do the same. Waiting for sex until marriage is possible. We can live holy lives before the Lord.

This doesn't mean the dream of marriage has gone away.

On August 21, 2004, I wrote:

Dear God,

You know my heart's desires. Lead me to my future husband. Mold me and make me a jewel to my husband's eyes. Bring our paths together. Mold him and make him a man after Your own heart. Lord, help me as I follow after You. Please give me a vision of what ministry You will have me be a part of. Help us both to stay pure and holy. Give us the strength we need to overcome temptation. Build us into warriors for You. Make us into Your disciples. My heart's desire is also to be a mother. Prepare me for that as well. Even at this moment I pray for my future children. I ask that they would serve You with all their hearts. I pray that our children will be witnesses of the gospel of Jesus Christ.

I give You my life, my husband and my children. I trust You with them.

I love You,
Sarah

On September 15, 2007, I wrote:

Lord, I trust You with my life. I trust You with my future and my dreams. I will wait for Your promises knowing that He who promised is faithful.

"For the vision is yet for an appointed time. . . . Though it tarries, wait for it; because it will surely come . . ." (Habakkuk 2:3, NKJV).

I realize You are in preparation for the things yet to come. Prepare me. Use me to glorify Your name. Let my life be a witness of Your love and faithfulness. Increase Your spirit inside of me. May my faith increase. Less of me and more of You. Let me know You with deep intimacy. Anoint Your servant for I am Your willing vessel.

When I dreamed of doing mission work, I never imagined it would be alone. When I dreamed of doing pastoral ministry, I thought I would be the pastor's wife—not the pastor. However, I wasn't going to stop fulfilling God's dream for my life because I was single.

I had to trust that I was in God's will. Therefore, being single must be God's will for my life, at least for this season of time. But for how much time? I'd hoped only a few years. But as I write this book, I'm 33 years old and still not married.

When I was considering writing a book, I thought I had to wait until I was married so I could have a "happily ever after" ending. God showed me that the "happily ever after" is about walking in obedience to God's leading—whether I'm married or single.

Are you living God's "happily ever after" for you?

Our Waiting Will Draw Us Closer to God.

"In her deep anguish Hannah prayed to the Lord, weeping bitterly."
—1 Samuel 1:10

Hannah was deeply troubled and poured out her soul to the Lord (v. 15). She wanted children, and her rival made it even harder for her to deal with her unrealized dreams. It never says that Hannah retaliated against her rival. The way she got rid of her grief was by praying and seeking the Lord.

"Trust in him at all times, O people; pour out your hearts to him for God is our refuge" (Psalm 62:8).

After Eli had told her to "go in peace and may the God of Israel grant you what you have asked of him" (1 Samuel 1:17), Hannah went her way and ate something. Her face was no longer downcast. She had prayed, and God had answered.

Even though she was not yet pregnant, she acted in faith that God had already answered her prayer. We also should take God at His word and act in faith. If we ask for something in prayer, we must believe that we will receive it. "Therefore I tell you, whatever you ask for in prayer, believe that you have received it, and it will be yours" (Mark 11:24).

Hannah did give birth. She had a son, Samuel, who was used mightily by God to lead Israel. She dedicated him to God as she had promised. I often wonder, "What if Hannah had not had to wait for children? Would she still have dedicated Samuel to God?"

God allows us to walk with unfulfilled dreams so that we appreciate them when they arrive. And we can be confident that it was only through God that they were fulfilled.

> **God allows us to walk with unfulfilled dreams so that we appreciate them when they arrive.**

"And we know that in all things God works for the good of those who love him, who have been called according to his purpose" (Romans 8:28).

God answered Hannah's prayer. God will never forget our prayers. He hears them and will answer them in His timing. He will do it in a way that will bring Him the most glory and honor. He also wants our hearts to be completely devoted to Him and love Him more than the answer to our prayer.

Proclaiming You and God

In 2009, my best friend wrote me several letters that I was to open during my first full mission term. She wrote me this note to open on my one-year anniversary in South Africa:

> *Today is Sept. 2, 2010—this marks your one year in South Africa! How things have changed! How your confidence in living in another country, in your God, in what God has called you to do has grown, and grown and grown!*
>
> *Undoubtedly, you may be wondering why God has not yet allowed any man in your life. I would*

imagine your thoughts must lurk in your mind. I know that you have told God you would give up having a husband if that was necessary to serve the Lord. It seems interesting to me to remember the high school days when you just wanted to marry a pastor. How amazing God showed you, you could be the pastor! You could be the leader among Master's Commission students, you could be the missionary to South Africa, you could travel miles and miles away by yourself with the Lord.

<u>It seems a pattern of God proclaiming you and Him</u>—[you and He] can do all things together—the hope and comfort in other people is false security—only He provides total and true protection, love and support. I have to admit, I think you would have missed out on many miracles and blessings of God had you relied on a husband. You would not be as strong in the Lord without them.

Regardless of what the future may hold—whether a husband is in the future or not—who better to spur youth on in purity than Sarah Careins! An adult who has and continues to walk the path of purity in all areas of life! What an encouragement and example you have been and will continue to be! I admire you! You are an inspiration of truly waiting on God—just as the song so dearly loved says, "I will serve you while I'm waiting. I will praise you while I'm waiting."[13] That you have done and more!

If the time should come when you are married, you will be giving a gift to someone that is priceless—beyond value—more precious than [the costliest] gems and jewels—you will be a pure blessing to someone— more than they ever thought possible!

"Don't let anyone look down on you because you are young, but set an example for the believers in

speech, in [life], in love, in faith and in purity" (1 Timothy 4:12).

"Your beauty should not come from outward adornment, such as elaborate hairstyles and the wearing of gold jewelry or fine clothes. Rather, it should be that of your inner self, the unfading beauty of a gentle and quiet spirit, which is of great worth in God's sight. For this is the way the holy women of the past who put their hope in God used to [make themselves beautiful]" (1 Peter 3:3–5a).

My friend was right. Being single on the mission field has taught me to rely on God like never before. Jesus is the love of my life. He will always be number one.

Our spouses should always be second to Jesus. No spouse will ever be perfect. They are not God. We cannot expect them to be God to us.

You don't have to feel like less of a person because you are not married. You and God together are more than enough. You don't have to wait for another person to "complete" you. Jesus completes us. God will empower you and help you.

Elisabeth Elliot said in her book *Passion and Purity*, "God knew that giving me _______ when I wanted him would not provide the far more important training I needed for things to come. It was in learning to eat that Living Bread, sufficient always for one day at a time . . . that I was taught and disciplined and prepared for later things."[14]

Seek God's Best

People may make comments like "you are too picky" or "you will never find a girl/guy like you want." Don't be discouraged by their negativity.

Trust God that His plans for you are the best. Walk in His will, and He'll take care of the desires of your heart (Psalm 37:3–4).

As you seek after the Lord, you will get closer and closer to Him. It is like you are climbing a spiritual ladder. The higher you climb this ladder, the farther away you get from more and more people. It may seem like you have fewer potential spouses to choose from. But that actually makes it easier to confirm which one is right for you!

Pete Wentz wrote the following poem:

Girls
are like apples
on trees. The best ones
are at the top of the tree.
The boys don't want to reach
for the good ones because they
are afraid of falling and getting hurt.
Instead, they get the rotten apples
from the ground that aren't as good,
but easy. So the apples up top think
something's wrong with them when in
reality they're amazing. They just
have to wait for the right boy to
come along, the one who's
brave enough to
climb all
the way
to the top
of the tree.

If you put finding a spouse over your relationship with God, you're on dangerous ground. The thing that's worse than being miserably single is being miserably married.

You need to know what you want in a guy or girl. Then when that person comes along, look at your list. Does he/she make the cut? I'm not talking about how tall they are or the color of their hair. At the top of the list should be "Believer in Jesus Christ." God has commanded His children not to be "unequally yoked" (2 Corinthians 6:14, NKJV). This means both of you love Jesus and will serve Him together.

Don't date a non-believer with the hopes that you will "save" them. Picture yourself standing on a chair and holding hands with someone below you. It's more likely that the person on the ground will pull you down with them than that you will pull them up.

Ask your pastor, family, and friends what they think about a potential spouse. They should be in agreement. If not, consider this as a possible warning sign. Always be careful because "love is blind."

Put Boundaries in Place

With physical intimacy, don't ask, "How far is too far? Where's the line?" If you ask this, it seems like you want to get as close to sin as possible without being guilty. Rather, try to stay as far away from the line as possible.

Remember that everyone is possibly someone else's future spouse until your actual wedding day. Therefore, you should treat them like a brother or sister. Don't do anything that you wouldn't do in front of your father—because your heavenly Father is watching you!

Song of Solomon 2:7 (NLT) says, "[Don't] awaken love until the time is right." It is best to keep the sleeping giant of our feelings asleep until the time God has appointed. These feelings are beautiful and from God. We should be careful not to put ourselves in situations that purposefully arouse them and lead us into temptation. This is why we should set boundaries in our lives. The Devil will try to lead you into temptation, but God always provides a way out (1 Corinthians 10:13). One way out is through the wisdom of boundaries.

Boundaries should be put in place before a decision needs to be made. This way you know your limits before you start crossing lines you never intended to.

For example, my best friend decided to save her first kiss for her wedding day. As she courted her future husband, they both understood this boundary. Now the Bible doesn't say, "Thou shall not kiss." However, she knew that a kiss would stir up feelings that could not be righteously fulfilled. So they waited to kiss. That first kiss on the wedding day was cherished and beautiful!

Sex is good in marriage. God created it! Sex is like a fire. In the fireplace (marriage), it can warm your house; you can cook with it and enjoy a nice book by the firelight. However, if it gets outside the fireplace (outside of God's purpose in marriage), the fire may burn you and destroy your entire house. Sex outside of marriage brings sexually transmitted diseases, abortions, hurt to families, and the list goes on and on.

What if you already went past the boundaries? Maybe you think of yourself as the rotten apple. Ask for God to forgive you and make you a new creation.

Therefore, if anyone is in Christ, the new creation has come: The old has gone, the new is here! All this is from God, who reconciled us to himself through Christ and gave us the ministry of reconciliation: that God was reconciling the world to himself in Christ, not counting people's sins against them. And he has committed to us the message of reconciliation. We are therefore Christ's ambassadors, as though God were making his

appeal through us. We implore you on Christ's behalf:
Be reconciled to God (2 Corinthians 5:17–20).
. . . Though your sins are like scarlet, they shall
be as white as snow; though they are red as crimson,
they shall be like wool (Isaiah 1:18b).

God longs to reconcile and restore you to His dream for your life. He wants to make you pure again. Leave your past behind and move forward. From this day on, choose to live in purity and wait for your future spouse.

Waiting with Jesus

Have you ever shaken a present to figure out what was in it?

Have you ever torn the paper off the corner of a gift to see what it was?

Sex is a gift from God for marriage. There is something beautiful about a wedding when you know the couple has waited. The excitement of opening the gift is still there. Other couples have stolen sexual pleasure by opening this gift before their wedding night.

While you wait, wait with Jesus. Become a jewel to be found! Make a commitment to your future spouse and your future children to wait for sex until your wedding day.

"Flee the evil desires of youth, and pursue righteousness, faith, love and peace, along with those who call on the Lord out of a pure heart" (2 Timothy 2:22).

Enjoy your singleness! You don't have to wash your husband's clothes or worry about paying your children's school fees. You are free to focus on serving the Lord.

You will never regret walking in purity. On your wedding day, you can tell your husband or wife, "I waited for you!"

Trusting in God's Timing

None of us knows the future. We don't know what God is preparing for us. Sometimes, it seems overwhelming and impossible to wait.

God gave me this word on May 18, 2015:

> *Ride the waves. You are not drowning or going to drown. Trust in Jesus. There will be a cost, but the Lord is with you. God's empowering you to handle every situation. He will give you wisdom. Your waiting on the Lord will not be disappointed. God is faithful. We don't know God's timing. He is orchestrating things behind the scenes that we don't see.*

We don't always see what God is doing, nor do we always understand the path that He has us take. We must trust in Jesus. Your waiting on the Lord will not be disappointed. God knows what is best for us. His timing is perfect.

As a Christian, we have to consider that God has possibly called us to a life of singleness (1 Corinthians 7:32–35). Paul lived a celibate life. I know that, for at least a season of my life, I have been called to singleness. However, I also wonder how a loving God would give me the desire for a family if it could not be fulfilled.

"Delight yourself . . . in the Lord, and He [will] give you the desires of your heart" (Psalm 37:4, NKJV).

I believe God will give you the grace and endurance to wait until the dreams of your heart can be fulfilled. Elisabeth Elliot said, "I do know that waiting on God requires the willingness to bear uncertainty, to carry within oneself the unanswered question, lifting the heart to God about it whenever it intrudes upon one's thoughts."[15]

Elisabeth's husband Jim Elliot said, "Wherever you are, be all there. Live to the hilt every situation you believe to be the will of God." If God has you in a season of singleness, don't fantasize about what could be. Be the best you can be where God has you.

While you wait on the Lord, keep serving Him, and believe for the fulfillment of the dream.

On May 3, 2011, I wrote:

> *Lord, today the hope of marriage seems to surround my thoughts. Honestly, I'm tired of feeling "physically" alone. I know You are always with me, but I'm asking for a helpmate. I know marriage will bring its challenges but I've also seen how it can be a blessing when it's in Your will. Lord, I only want Your will. I want a marriage that will bring glory to God. A marriage that will be a testimony of Your faithfulness and love.*
>
> *I ask that You would bring our paths together. I don't want to pursue anything or try to create it. I want to know that it was Your hand that brought us together. I want to be sure that it's Your perfect will. I will wait for Your perfect will but I ask that you would not delay and help me to wait. Guard my heart and my thoughts.*
>
> *I pray that our hearts' desire to serve You would be unified. Lord, You have shown me that missions is my calling so I ask that You would also show my future spouse.*
>
> *I pray that he would be a man full of the Holy Spirit, willing and ready to serve in any way You call him to. May he be a man I will respect and who will lead our family well. I pray that You would guide him*

and me toward godly character and the calling that is Your dream for our lives.

Lord, thank you that You are faithful to grant us the desires of our hearts. I wait with expectation."

I love Elisabeth Elliot's story, but her story is her story. My story is my story. Your story is your story. Follow God, His Word, and listen to the Holy Spirit. Don't try to live someone else's life. Live your life. Wait on God's timing, but when the moment is right, don't be afraid to live God's dream.

The Lord gave me this word on January 2, 2016. Now I proclaim it over your life: "Don't get frustrated that you can't figure out the next 10 or 20 years. Obey and go. Your journey is going to be amazing."

"The Lord makes firm the steps of the one who delights in him" (Psalm 37:23).

"In all your ways submit to him, and he will make your paths straight" (Proverbs 3:6).

"Rejoice always, pray continually, give thanks in all circumstances; for this is God's will for you in Christ Jesus" (1 Thessalonians 5:16–18).

Expect God to guide you toward His purpose for your life. Don't walk in frustration, but thank the Lord for His perfect will and timing.

Are you willing to wait for God's fulfillment of the dream?

Will you trust that God's timing is perfect?

Will you serve Him while you are waiting?

Will you obey and go even when you can't figure out the future?

CHAPTER ELEVEN

JUST WHEN YOU THOUGHT YOU'D FIGURED IT OUT . . . (DREAMS ON THE ALTAR)

"Whoever wants to be my disciple must deny themselves and take up their cross daily and follow me."
—Luke 9:23

What do you love more? The dream or God? Just as Abraham was willing to lay down his son Isaac on the altar, we must also lay down our dreams. In fact, sometimes our dreams have to die daily—not just once.

I remember when God first called me to be a missionary. I laid my life on God's altar then. But even now, years later, there are still moments when I have to go to the altar and be willing to lay it all down at Jesus' feet again. Answering the call to follow Christ is sometimes a daily choice.

Therefore, I urge you, brothers and sisters, in view of God's mercy, to offer your bodies as a living sacrifice, holy and pleasing to God—this is your true and proper worship. Do not conform to the pattern of this world, but be transformed by the renewing of your mind. Then you will be able to test and approve what God's will is—his good, pleasing and perfect will (Romans 12:1–2).

In Chapter Three, I mention that we are called to be a living sacrifice. This implies a continual sacrifice that never ends. Our lives are to be laid on the altar daily, not just on a Sunday or when the pastor preaches a nice message.

The altar was the place where animals were sacrificed with fire in Old Testament times. If we are living sacrifices, the altar is not going to be comfortable. It might even hurt a little.

God likes to move us out of our comfort zones. Each time I began to get comfortable, or just when I thought I had figured out how to do everything, God always changed things. He wants us to continually rely on Him, not ourselves, as our source of strength and provision.

When you deny yourself, you begin to dream beyond yourself.

When you deny yourself, you begin to dream beyond yourself.

Identity

When we are growing up, we all want to know what we will become. Will I be a missionary, author, teacher, artist, pastor's wife, or [insert your childhood dream here]?

At one point, after years of trying to figure it out, I thought I had found my identity: Sarah Careins is a missionary to Africa. I began to wrap my identity around my job description rather than my God.

Ultimately, your identity is found in being God's child—not in the accomplishment of the dream. More important than the fact that I serve as a missionary in South Africa is my identity as God's daughter.

Too many of us get caught up in our job descriptions. When we are asked to introduce ourselves, we say, "Hi. I'm Sarah Careins. I train youth leaders and pioneer university ministry in South Africa." Imagine if we instead introduced ourselves like this: "Hi. I'm Sarah Careins, a daughter of the King of Kings and Lord of all Lords." Now that's an introduction!

In Luke 20, Jesus was asked if it was okay to pay taxes. Jesus answered, "Whose portrait and inscription are on [a coin]?" It was Caesar's image. Jesus said to them in verse 25, "Then give back to Caesar what is Caesar's, and to God what is God's."

The coin had Caesar's identity on it, but you and I are made in the image of God. Scripture says to "give . . . to God what is God's." In essence, we are called to give God what is due Him. His image is upon us, and we owe Him ourselves.

When giving an offering, many people focus on the money, but I often picture putting myself in the offering plate. My life is a sacrifice to God. It includes my finances, future, and dreams.

Are you holding anything back? Is there anything that you are not willing to release into God's offering plate?

Anything that you put above your relationship with God can become an idol. These are not always bad things. They may even include the dream that God has given you. Do you look to the dream for your joy or to God?

In recent years, God has taught me that I can make Africa an idol in my life. For years, I dreamed of going to Africa. Then God brought me here, and the journey has been incredible. At the same time, God has gently whispered to me, "Am I more important to you than your African dream?"

On July 14, 2015, I wrote these words:

> *My favorite quotation has always been "Dream so big that you will fail so that, when you succeed, you will know it was God." Lord, I've dreamed BIG! You've proven Yourself time and again. You gave me Africa. I lay my dreams of Africa on the altar. I lay my dreams of marriage on Your altar. I lay my desire to be with my family and friends on the altar. What I desire is You!"*

True success is when God is glorified, not "self." My heart's desire, above everything else, should be to know God and let His glory be known by others. I must put self on the altar.

Thomas Hale, missionary to Nepal, said, "The biggest hindrance to the missionary task is self. Self that refuses to die. Self that refuses to sacrifice. Self that refuses to give. Self that refuses to go."

Wherever God calls me, I will go. Whatever God calls me to sacrifice, I will give.

Are you dreaming beyond self?

Are you willing to lay your dreams on the altar?

Pursuing God's Dream

Where is God leading me? What am I going to do with my life? These are questions each of us has at some point in our lives. The truth is that God is more concerned about who we are becoming than where we are going. God wants us to grow out of our independence and into dependence on Him. Pursuing God's dream for your life is a walk of faith into the unknown.

God promised Abraham that he would have a son (Genesis 12). Abraham waited and waited for this dream to come true—for 25 years. Finally, his wife, Sarah, gave birth to their promised son, Isaac, in their old age.

God gave Abraham his dream of Isaac, but then God asked for Isaac back. Why would God give someone a promise and then ask for it back? Read Genesis 22:1–3a, 9–13:

> *Some time later God tested Abraham. He said to him, "Abraham!"*
>
> *"Here I am," he replied.*
>
> *Then God said, "Take your son, your only son, whom you love—Isaac—and go to the region of Moriah. Sacrifice him there as a burnt offering on a mountain I will show you."*
>
> *Early the next morning Abraham got up and loaded his donkey. He took with him two of his servants and his son Isaac. . . .*
>
> *When they reached the place God had told him about, Abraham built an altar there and arranged the wood on it. He bound his son Isaac and laid him on the altar, on top of the wood. Then he reached out his hand and took the knife to slay his son. But the angel of the Lord called out to him from heaven, "Abraham! Abraham!"*
>
> *"Here I am," he replied.*
>
> *"Do not lay a hand on the boy," he said. "Do not do anything to him. Now I know that you fear God, because you have not withheld from me your son, your only son."*

> *Abraham looked up and there in the thicket he saw a*
> *ram caught by its horns. He went over and took the ram*
> *and sacrificed it as a burnt offering instead of his son.*

When Abraham was called by God in Genesis 12, he had to leave the familiar and go to a land unknown. He had to leave everything that could provide security and instead trust in God. But the call to sacrifice Isaac in Genesis 22 was different. Genesis 12 called Abraham to leave his past; Genesis 22 called him to leave his future!

Phil Vischer, the creator of VeggieTales, had a big idea that grew to an $11.5 million net worth. Then he went bankrupt and lost everything. This is what God taught him:

> *What does it mean when God gives you a dream and*
> *the dream comes to life and God shows up and without*
> *warning the dream dies? . . . If God gives a person a*
> *dream, breathes life into it and then it dies then God*
> *might want to know what is more important to the*
> *person—the dream or God . . . God learned . . . that*
> *Abraham would let go of everything before he would*
> *let go of God . . . God said, "Ok, now I can use you."*
> *Why would God want us to let go of our dreams?*
> *Because anything that you are unwilling to let go of is*
> *an idol and you are in sin. . . . Rather than finding my*
> *identity in my relationship with God, I was finding*
> *it in my intense drive to do good works.*[16]

The impact God has planned for us does not occur when we are pursuing it. It occurs when we are pursuing God. God knows the plan. He knows the strategy. So let go of the outcomes and put your plans in God's hands and let Him direct your steps.

When God gives me a vision, He never tells me every

step ahead of time. He wants us to trust Him for each step of the journey.

Will you let go of your dream?

Making an Ishmael

Abraham's faith was strong in Genesis 22, but he had learned some lessons on the journey to get there. In Genesis 16, he made a mistake. In fact, he made an Ishmael. Instead of putting the dream on the altar and letting God take care of the fulfillment, Abraham and Sarah (Abram and Sarai) thought they could help God's plan.

> *Now Sarai, Abram's wife, had borne him no children. But she had an Egyptian slave named Hagar; so she said to Abram, "The Lord has kept me from having children. Go, sleep with my slave; perhaps I can build a family through her." Abram agreed to what Sarai said (Genesis 16:1–2).*

Sarah and Abraham thought that they could help God's vision happen by Abraham sleeping with Hagar. Abraham could have said, "Sarah, I love you, and I wouldn't take anyone other than you. God promised He would give us a son—so we need to wait on God's promise." But instead of waiting on God's timing, Abraham tried to hurry the plan. This resulted in strife in his marriage and the mistreatment of Hagar.

In the midst of all of this, God took care of Hagar and her son Ishmael. Genesis 16:7 says the angel of the Lord found Hagar in the desert and encouraged her. Hagar recognized "the God who sees me" (v. 13). Even Hagar had to trust God with her future dreams.

Galatians 4:29 (NLT) says that Ishmael was born "by human effort" and Isaac was born "by the power of the

Spirit." As we pursue God's vision, we must allow the dream to be birthed in the Spirit. Don't try to create it yourself. Give it to God. Put it on the altar.

Abraham waited 25 years from the promise until its fulfillment in Isaac. Then God asked him to sacrifice Isaac, his dream. This time, Abraham had faith to obey God with action. He understood that you should do whatever God says.

God wants to know that you fear Him. The word "fear" means respect, awe, love and submission to God.

Abraham had faith, but we often overlook Isaac's faith. Imagine your father putting you on an altar as a sacrifice. If I were Isaac, I would have screamed for dear life! But somehow this old man bound a young Isaac and placed him on the altar. The son must have cooperated. Isaac didn't understand why, but he trusted his father.

Abraham had learned through Ishmael to love God more than the dream. He had learned that God is capable of the impossible. Abraham believed that God would provide a way to fulfill His promise through Isaac—even if He had to raise him from the dead (Hebrews 11:19).

But God didn't need to raise Isaac from the dead because, at the very last minute, He provided a ram in the thicket for the sacrifice. Abraham called that place, "the Lord will provide" (Genesis 22:14).

God is never late. He is seldom early. He is always on time.

We won't always understand *why*. Abraham thought he had figured it all out. The dream was complete. Isaac had been born. Yet, there was still a test. God wanted to know that Abraham loved Him more than Isaac.

God never puts us through a test that we won't pass. Have faith in the Father who does have it all figured out.

Will you submit your dreams to God?

Will you love God more than the dream?

El Salvador or Adam Moments

I've known my best friend since kindergarten. As children, we lived about two miles away from each other in a small farming community. There was a bridge over a stream between our homes where we often met. I would ride my bicycle, and she would sometimes ride her horse.

She loved horses, but she loved God more. As soon as she finished high school, she sold her horse to help pay for the cost of going to El Salvador to work in an orphanage. She has always had a passion for missions.

After spending six months in El Salvador, she returned to the United States to finish her degree at a university. Her dream was to serve God by working with children and was willing to go anywhere in the world. Then she met Adam. She was one of those girls who never wanted to get married. She had plans to be single and do great things for God. But meeting Adam complicated things.

Before committing to marry Adam, my friend returned to El Salvador for a month. During this time, she prayed for direction and wisdom from God. She was willing to serve as a missionary in El Salvador and leave America and Adam behind. Instead, God encouraged her to marry Adam.

Today she is not a missionary to El Salvador, but she is a witness to the world from Muncie, Indiana. She serves as the children's director at her local church. Both she and Adam invite international students to their home and share the love of God with them. They financially support orphans around the world through the Boaz Project. In the midst of her busyness, she takes the time to encourage her missionary friend in South Africa (yes, me). This is the heart of God. This is living in obedience to God's call.

God asked my friend to live in Indiana. God asked me to live in South Africa.

God's plan sometimes looks different than what we imagine. We must always remember that His plan is the best one for our lives. Every life is different. No testimony is the same, but the result is always the proclamation of God's name.

"Many are the plans in a person's heart, but it is the LORD's purpose that prevails" (Proverbs 19:21).

We can trust that God's plan will happen, though we don't always see the results right away. There are different seasons in life. Some of us might be in winter. The tree is dormant, and we cannot yet see the fruit.

When you are connected to Jesus, the Vine, your ministry will be fruitful. Don't be discouraged when you don't see the fruit right away. There will be long-term effects that we will only see in Heaven.

By living close to Jesus, you will be able to hear when God calls you to leave El Salvador or go to South Africa. You cannot live *for* Jesus if you don't live *from* Jesus, abiding in the Vine. In fact, you cannot truly live until you die to yourself.

When God Changes Things

"Yet he [Abraham] did not waver through unbelief regarding the promise of God, but was strengthened in his faith and gave glory to God."
—Romans 4:20

There comes a point when God stops telling you what to do because you should know what to do. By the time he was called to give up Isaac, Abraham had lived long enough to have faith and know the promises of God. His faith was strong, and he gave God the glory.

There are other points when you think you know what you're doing, but then God changes things. Our lives must remain flexible; we must always be willing to lay it all down.

In 2014, I moved into a new home in South Africa. This was the first time in my life that I had ever been allowed to paint the walls of a house just the way I wanted. After a lot of work, the house felt like my home. In this moment of peace, God reminded me to "hold onto this lightly." My home is not mine. I am only a temporary resident. Any furniture or other material possessions I accumulate may all need to be sold in an instant.

At the end of that year, I watched as my mentors and friends Wayne and Delight Peercy sold all their possessions in Africa and moved back to the United States. God had called them to transition into another season. They were in God's will coming to South Africa, and they were in God's will leaving.

Our real home is in Heaven. The places we live on this earth will always be temporary. We cannot take our possessions with us to Heaven. We should always be willing to let go of everything at any season of our lives. "In the same way, those of you who do not give up everything you have cannot be my disciples" (Luke 14:33).

Are you prepared and ready for the fulfillment of the dream?

Are you doing everything you know to do now?

Are you willing to change and do something different if God asks?

Chinese Fortune Cookies

A Chinese fortune cookie is a crisp cookie usually made from flour, sugar, vanilla, and sesame seed oil with a piece of paper inside—a "fortune"—on which is written a general truth or vague "prophecy."

In 2006, I taped five small pieces of paper from Chinese fortune cookies in my journal. Now, I believe in what God says and don't want to promote horoscopes or fortune tellers. We need to seek our answers from God—not a cookie. But these five sayings held a lot of biblical truth for me:

Cookie #1:
All the darkness in the world cannot put out
a single candle.

The light God has placed in you has a purpose—to shine! When light enters a room, darkness has to flee. God is calling each of us to let the light of Jesus shine through us (Matthew 5:16).

Cookie #2:
You will step on the soil of many countries.

God has called us to go and make disciples of all nations (Matthew 28:19–20). Be willing to go wherever God opens the doors for you (Colossians 4:3; Ephesians 6:19).

Cookie #3:
All the effort you are making will ultimately pay off.

God sees your sacrifice (Romans 12:1). You will receive an eternal reward (Hebrews 6:10).

Cookie #4:
All the answers you need are right there in front of you!

Sometimes we ask God for answers, but they are right in front of us. Most of these answers are in His Word, the Holy Bible (Psalm 119:105). We need to hear His voice through the Word and prayer.

Cookie #5:
Adventure is not outside; it is within.

More than what you do with your life, God is interested in who you are becoming (Ephesians 2:8–9).

As we take the focus off of ourselves and put it on God, the Lord is able to take us farther than we ever imagined. Hold onto the promises that God has spoken over your life, "being confident of this, that he who began a good work in you will carry it on to completion until the day of Christ Jesus" (Philippians 1:6).

Dreams Too Small

"If the Great Commission is true, our plans are not too big; they are too small."
—Pat Morely

God's desire is for you to dream big dreams that are beyond yourself. They should be so big that they are impossible without God's help.

Huldah Buntain, missionary to India, was asked how she and her husband, Mark, were able to accomplish so much for the Kingdom of God. She answered:

We took it one day at a time. We worked hard and did our best to listen to the voice of the Lord, knowing that He was the One who sent us. He was the One who performed the miracles and He was the One who sustained us.

In your journey to know God and make God known, take it one day at a time. Work hard. Listen to the voice of the Lord. Know that God has sent you. God will perform the miracles. God will sustain you on the journey.

David Livingstone said, "This generation can only reach this generation." God has placed you on earth for "such a time as this" (Esther 4:14). You will be able to reach people that I can never reach. I will reach people that you can never reach. Each of us has a part to play on God's "dream team."

Don't hold onto your own dreams for your life. Release them onto the altar. Your dreams are too small. God wants to give you something even greater.

Are your dreams too small?

Do you love God more than the dream?

Will you lay your dreams on the altar?

CHAPTER TWELVE
THE BIG HOUSE
(DREAMS FULFILLED)

*"Therefore go and make disciples of all nations,
baptizing them in the name of the Father and of the
Son and of the Holy Spirit, and teaching them to obey
everything I have commanded you. And surely I am
with you always, to the very end of the age."*
—Matthew 28:19–20

God's fulfillment of His dream comes in two parts. Part
one is your salvation. Part two is you making disciples
who make disciples. This is the legacy we leave for
others. This is the fulfillment of God's dream for you.

The Great Commission in Matthew 28:19–20 says
to go and make "disciples," not "converts." Some people assume that this passage was written for pastors or
missionaries. The Great Commission was given to all

believers. If you believe in Jesus Christ as your Lord and Savior, you are not only called to be a disciple. You are also called to make disciples.

The word "disciple" actually means "learner." Jesus and Paul took this meaning a step further to mean "a learner who accepts the teaching of Christ, not only in belief but also in lifestyle."[17]

God wants more than "believers." Even the Devil believes that there is a God. God wants transformation.

It is not without significance that the word "disciple" occurs in the New Testament 294 times, "Christian" only 3 times, and "believers" only 7 times. We are called to more than just going to church on Sundays. We are called to more than just making sure we get to Heaven. We are called to make disciples so that others can also reach Heaven!

The Great Commission says that making disciples includes baptizing them and teaching them to obey Jesus' commands. Jesus' message was a call to discipleship—not to faith alone but to faith and obedience. Obedience does not achieve salvation, but it is evidence of it.

Discipleship is not just a Bible study class on Wednesday nights. It is a lifestyle change. It won't be easy. Salvation is free, but discipleship will cost you everything.[18]

"The time has come," he said. "The kingdom of God has come near. Repent and believe the good news!"

As Jesus walked beside the Sea of Galilee, he saw Simon and his brother Andrew casting a net into the lake, for they were fishermen. "Come, follow me," Jesus said, "and I will send you out to fish for people." At once they left their nets and followed him.

When he had gone a little farther, he saw James son of Zebedee and his brother John in a boat, preparing their nets. Without delay he called them, and they left their father Zebedee in the boat with the hired men and followed him (Mark 1:15–20).

We must be willing to leave everything we have known to follow Christ without delay. Simon and his brother left their nets, their fishing business. James and John left their father to follow Jesus. As for me, I want to do God's will no matter the cost.

Jesus began the work, but He uses his disciples to complete it. Today we are his disciples. Each of us has a part to play in God's dream. We must be obedient to fulfill it.

"My food," said Jesus, "is to do the will of him who sent me and to finish his work" (John 4:34).

Our job is to finish God's work, to fulfill the dream.

Those who introduce others to Jesus and lead them to the point of accepting Christ are doing something of eternal significance. The one thing that will give you the most satisfaction in life is seeing souls saved!

Everyone has a part to play. Each of our roles is different. Ultimately, it is God who will make the seed of salvation grow. "I planted the seed, Apollos watered it, but God has been making it grow" (1 Corinthians 3:6).

Discipleship empowers others to accomplish God's dreams for their own lives. Barnabas saw the potential in Saul/Paul and helped him grow in ministry. Eventually, Paul discipled Timothy and did the same for him. Timothy went on to disciple others.

As a missionary, my job is to work myself out of a job. I'm sent to a foreign land to start work and train the nationals in how to carry it on without me. I know I've done my job when I don't have a job to do anymore. However, there is always more work to do in God's Kingdom, so I'm never really out of a job.

The joy of discipleship is seeing all your hard work and invested time reproduced in another disciple.

The joy of discipleship is seeing all your hard work and invested time reproduced in another disciple.

Are you making disciple-makers? Are you working yourself out of a job?

Your Other Name

Growing up, I loved that my name, Sarah, means "princess." What little girl doesn't want to be a princess? However, Sarah also has another meaning that I didn't embrace until I came to Africa: "mother of nations." In the Bible, Sarah was Abraham's wife. God changed her name to mean "mother of nations." In the year 2010, some of my African friends wanted to give me an African name. The more they thought about it, the more they liked "Masechaba" which means "mother of nations" in Sepedi. This has become my name in South Africa. If you yell out "Masechaba," I'll turn and look to see if you are talking to me.

When I'm introduced to one of my African brothers or sisters, they usually tell me, "Hi, my name is Mpho, but you can call me Gift," or "My name is Nthabiseng, but you can call me Thabi." They feel that their African name is too hard for me to pronounce, so they try to shorten it or give me the English translation. So whenever I introduce myself in Africa, I say, "Hi. I'm Sarah, but you can call me Masechaba." I win their friendship immediately. They want to know how a white lady could get such a name.

Though I don't have any biological children yet, God has blessed me with many spiritual children. The name Masechaba reminds me that I am a mother of nations. God is calling me to train up His children in the way they should go. The hard part is being willing to release them and get out of the way so they can learn from their own failures and successes. Like a real mom, I have to let them grow up and move away from me. But it's a proud moment when I see the fruit of their lives impacting others.

My prayer is that we would all be mothers and fathers of nations.

Is This Road Even on the GPS?

No journey is perfect. There will be bumps in the road. In Africa, there tend to be a lot of potholes. Some roads are paved and easy to travel. Others are dirt, and you may wonder if the GPS took you down the wrong path.

In some cases, the GPS doesn't even recognize the road you are following. You are trying to follow the directions given by a national ("turn at the tree and then at the third big set of rocks go left"). But as you guide your car through a herd of cows, villagers look at you like, "What does this white lady think she is doing here?"

Eventually, you end up at the destination. Your journey is complete. It may not have looked like you planned . . . but you did get there.

Every disciple has a journey. No one has the same story as anyone else.

Someone may get saved and the next day lead their friend to the Lord. They just started the discipleship journey but have already made a disciple. The first disciple teaches their friend what they learned the day before.

Another person might accept Christ and begin their own journey of knowing God but not realize for months or years that they also need to share this good news with their friends and family.

Others may think they have to earn a Bible degree or become perfect before making a disciple, which is untrue. You don't have to be perfect to make disciples. Only Jesus is perfect. You just need to be willing and obedient.

Then there are those Christians who have been saved for 20 years, and if you asked them, "Who have you discipled?" they wouldn't be able to tell you one name because they think that is why the church pays the pastor. They assume discipleship is the pastor's job. However, the pastor's job is to equip the church congregation to fulfill God's dream—which is to make disciples. This is sad to me because many believers haven't even tried to make a disciple. They are living in disobedience to God's command: "go and make disciples."

It's not about the number of people you reach. It's about the obedience.

It's not about the number of people you reach. It's about the obedience.

There is a story of a man who had only one disciple his whole life. But that disciple impacted someone else who impacted someone else who impacted thousands. I believe that when God accounts for this man's fruit, He will count not the one but the multiplied seed—thousands.

Robert H. Schuller once said, "Anyone can count the seeds in an apple, but only God can count the number of apples in a seed."

What Is the Evidence of Discipleship in Your Life?

The first step to being a disciple-maker is to be a disciple. Are you a disciple of Christ? If you were taken to court and put on trial, would there be enough evidence to prove that you are a disciple?

Exhibit A—**Fruit**
*"If you remain in me and my words remain in you,
ask whatever you wish, and it will be done for you.
This is to my Father's glory, that you bear much fruit,
showing yourself to be my disciples."*
—John 15:7–8

The evidence of someone's discipleship is their fruit. "Fruit" refers to their character. Do they have the fruit of the Spirit (Galatians 5:22–23)? The fruit of the Spirit is not just about you; it's also about how you treat others. What effect do you have on other people?

Exhibit B—**Love**
*"A new command I give you: Love one another.
As I have loved you, so you must love one another.
By this everyone will know that you are my disciples,
if you love one another."*
—John 13:34–35

How will you know if someone is a disciple? By their love for others and for one another. Do you only love yourself or do you truly love others? If you are always talking badly about other people in the church, how is this a witness to non-believers? If you are not loving, why would a sinner want what you have?

Exhibit C—**Sacrifice**
*"[T]hose of you who do not give up everything you
have cannot be my disciples."*
—Luke 14:33

Are you willing to give it all up? God may not make you give everything, but if He asked you to, would you be willing? Do you love God more than everything else? Today a lot of people want both the world and God. The test of a real disciple is whether you would give up everything to follow Jesus.

Exhibit D—**Commitment/Obedience**

"To the Jews who had believed him, Jesus said, 'If you hold to my teaching, you are really my disciples. Then you will know the truth, and the truth will set you free.'"
—John 8:31–32

The evidence of a true disciple is that you are committed and obey the Word. Are you someone God can count on? Is your disobedience a disappointment to God and others? Are you a slave to your lack of commitment?

Jesus is the way, the *truth*, and the life. He said that "you will know the *truth*, and the *truth* will set you free." When knowing Jesus is a priority in our lives, we find freedom. We find freedom to be committed to a cause that is worth fighting for. We are obedient out of love for Jesus—not out of obligation to a religion.

Exhibit E—**Fishers of People**

"'Come, follow me,' Jesus said, 'and I will send you out to fish for people.'"
—Matthew 4:19

When you follow Jesus, you prove that you are His disciple by "fishing" for others. Jesus loves to use terms that people understand. Peter and Andrew were fishermen. He called them to "fish" for people rather than worldly dreams.

Jesus calls each of us to a higher dream: to influence others for God and lead them to Christ. No matter what your job is today, if you are not striving in some way to introduce others to Christ, then you are not doing the most important work that God has called you to do.

Be the Church

In my first few years in South Africa, I focused on training youth leaders in local churches. I taught them how to connect an unsaved young person with the local church, then how to disciple those youths to become healthy leaders who would take other unsaved young people through the same process.

Eventually, I would even train other trainers to teach these same concepts of discipleship to grow our youth ministries across South Africa. For the church to grow, there must be disciples who make disciples. This concept of true discipleship is still growing among our churches.

I believe that God is raising up a generation of young people who will be disciple-makers and dream beyond themselves. Are you ready to dream beyond yourself?

There are times when I get tired of "church" ("religion" may be a better word). Even Jesus was tired of the Pharisees and Sadducees, the hypocrites of His day. They had the appearance of following God, but they were not living out the love of God in their daily lives.

A healthy church loves people. Jesus spent a lot of time with His disciples, but He also spent time with sinners—the people no one else cared for.

I'm not saying we should forsake the church. We need to *be* the church. The body of Christ should encourage us to have fellowship with other disciples, but we cannot remain in an isolated "Christian bubble." God calls us to be the light in the darkness. We shine brighter in dark places.

Please understand: if you are a recovering alcoholic, this does not mean you need to go into bars to reach sinners. We need to walk in wisdom and holiness. Resist temptation and set an example for others to follow.

"Show me your friends, and I'll show you your future" is a saying that I've heard a lot. It means that if your closest friends are living a life of destruction, you will most likely follow the same path. When you spend a lot of time with people, you start to talk like them and act like them. This is why our closest friends should be other disciples who encourage us and keep us accountable. If they act like Jesus, then we will act like Jesus.

God may ask us to leave behind some friends from the past. God will bring other people to witness to them. It's not our job to save everyone. We need to place some people in God's hands so that we can become the disciples we need to be.

At the same time, we must not neglect to spend time with sinners and show them the love of Jesus. We should all have some friends who are not yet saved. Be a real friend. Let your love for Jesus rub off on them instead of them bringing you down.

Who are your friends?

A Ripe Harvest Field

While helping develop the National Youth Ministries, I realized that there was a huge harvest field on the university campuses of South Africa. In South African culture, a person is considered a "youth" if they are between the ages of 15 and 35, as long as they are still single. This means that at many of our youth camps, I was meeting university students.

In 2011 and 2012, I hosted a mission team from a university ministry in Fort Wayne, Indiana. The mission team trained in evangelism at the local church, held assemblies at elementary and high schools, witnessed in the hospital, and conducted outreaches at the university and in the community surrounding the local church. During these times of ministry, God spoke clearly to me.

We held our final event at an outdoor amphitheater called Thami Square at the University of Limpopo campus. Under the stars of the African sky, our local church members and mission team led this outreach. The program included live music, dancing, drama, prizes, and testimonies. The evening ended with a short message and a response time for students to accept Jesus Christ into their lives.

As the outreach leader, I was busy assisting the altar workers. I didn't plan to pray with students. However, some of the mission team members asked me to help pray with a girl for salvation. Her name was Veniesha. After leading her in the sinner's prayer, I felt like we should also pray for her to be baptized in the Holy Spirit. I quickly explained to her what this meant, and she agreed that she would like to receive this. Within a minute of praying for her, she began to pray in tongues. It was one of the most glorious moments in my ministry.

The Lord used Veniesha to speak to my heart about how students are ready to receive Christ and walk in the power of the Holy Spirit. They only need someone to go and share the love of Jesus with them.

I visited with Veniesha for several weeks. I gave her a Bible, prayed with her, and introduced her to the local church. When the semester ended, she went back home, and I had to return to the USA. When I came back to South Africa, I couldn't find her. I wasn't able to follow up with her anymore and make sure she became a true disciple and not just a convert. Did I fail to make a disciple?

There have been times when I wasn't able to follow through with discipleship. I lost track of the person. This is not ideal. God calls us to make disciples, not just converts. Yet God knows every situation. I have to trust that God has their lives in His hands. He will bring other people along their paths to complete their discipleship journey. God's dream will be fulfilled in their lives! I may plant the seed, another may water it, but God will make sure it grows. The important question is this: am I walking in obedience to God and doing what I can to fulfill the dream?

The Big House

By 2014, I had handed most of the work of the National Youth Ministry over to other leaders. God had put on my heart the need to pioneer a university ministry. We later called this The Journey.

At first, it seemed like every door closed on me. I initially thought I would go to a certain campus, but then God opened the door to another network of campuses.

These were not the big fancy universities that everyone wanted to attend. Some of the facilities had been neglected. Students would often strike for free education, which disrupted the exam schedules. Some shacks sold alcohol and promised a party every night—right outside one campus' gate.

Just as some cities have many churches, there are universities in South Africa that give students the opportunity to attend many different churches or Christian organizations. But I soon realized that the places where God had opened doors for me were overlooked. Few churches had even attempted to reach these students. They had been spiritually ignored and confused.

Some of the so-called "churches" did not preach the gospel of Jesus. At one campus, a "pastor" had told students to eat grass and drink petrol to prove the power of God in their lives. Because of this, students no longer felt that they could trust the church.

As the students and I walked and prayed on this campus, I felt God saying that those teachings were sinking sand. We needed to preach Christ because He would be the solid rock. When hard times came for these students, their faith would not waiver because they would know the truth of Jesus.

One day, we had our information table set up on one of the most neglected campuses, talking to students. The only other "church" represented that day believed that Jesus had already come back a second time as a Zulu man named Shembe. These false teachings were confusing students about what was true and what was a lie.

While I was walking to the car to get something, a young man asked if he could speak with me. For almost an hour, he asked me a lot of questions about faith. Eventually, I was able to pray with him to receive Christ. His name is Thabelo.[19]

After praying with him, I invited Thabelo to go to church with us on Sunday. He did! The following day, I woke up thinking that I should give him the opportunity to be water baptized. So that very week, we announced that a water Baptism service would be held on Saturday. Eight students chose to make their faith public by being water baptized.

Before being baptized, Thabelo shared his testimony, stating that he was like the Ethiopian and I was like Philip in Acts 8. On the day of his salvation, I had simply explained the Scriptures to him. Now nothing would stop him from being baptized in water.

Since that day, we have learned more about Thabelo's struggles and triumphs. During one of our Bible studies, students were asked to draw a picture depicting their life journey. Most students drew a road map, but Thabelo drew a village. He had small huts surrounding the outer circle of the village with tombstones next to each one. He stated that his whole life he'd gone from place to place and only found death and darkness. Then he showed us the "big house" he'd drawn in the middle of the village. There were no tombstones, and he had drawn windows on the house. He explained that now he is in the big house with light and no death!

As I write this, Thabelo is still on his discipleship journey. He faithfully attends almost every Bible study on campus. It has been a joy to see his faith grow. I believe that God will continue to work in his life and use him to help others on their faith journeys.

A Word of Encouragement

One disciple-maker who is a big encourager is Regaogetswe. He is a student at one of our universities and grew up attending one of the national churches that I partner with.

When we began pioneering this ministry, Regaogetswe was one of the first students to join us for prayer walks and Bible studies. He has seen The Journey grow from only a few students meeting outside on a picnic table to God's provision of a small room and then an even bigger one. He remembers when just a few of us prayed over the hall on campus, asking that it would one day be filled with students worshipping God. Then he saw our prayers come to life as we hosted two different movie nights and saw over two hundred students attend and several receive Christ.

Regaogetswe is also a disciple who makes disciples. He seeks out other students on campus to befriend them, leads a small group Bible study, and meets with others to talk about their relationships with Jesus.

On the 28th of November, 2015, I received this message from Regaogetswe:

After yesterday's exam, I felt like packing what is mine here and going back home. I was so discouraged. When I arrived at my place, I went straight to bed and slept the whole six hours. I didn't want to face the world again. I just wanted to sleep for long. But I remembered something you once shared with us that years back you'd feel so discouraged when things didn't add up and want to pack and go home.

As the year comes to an end, I just want to thank you, pastor, for all your teachings. You taught me not to give up nor give in, so that at the end of the day, I'll say, "I've fought the good fight and I have finished the course, I have kept the faith." We really learn a lot from your passion. You don't only teach us but you practice what you are preaching. I really don't know why you chose South Africa. Why you chose Gauteng Province? Why you chose [this university]? Why you chose The Journey? Most importantly, why you chose us? . . . But I know that God's plans are not ours, neither are His ways our ways.

We really appreciate you in our lives. May the good Lord keep doing wonders in you and through you, Pastor Sarah.

My reply to his message was:

Wow! Thank you so much for sharing this with me. God is amazing because on my own I would have never met you, but God knows exactly what each of us needs. He really does guide our paths.

Don't give up. Don't be discouraged. Do your best and leave the rest to God. Sometimes He can even turn what we imagine are failures into a blessing. We look back and realize God was teaching us and guiding us in our journey.

May God continue to remind you of His plans and purposes for your life. I see greatness in you and know that God will accomplish much in you and through you! Hold on. Press through. Seek the Lord. It is only in knowing God that we are able to fight because we know He fights for us. We are never alone and His plan will prevail!

God will orchestrate your life to impact certain people at certain times. Why go one place and not another? God knows. We must listen to His leading and do our part in fulfilling His dreams.

As I took steps of faith to come to South Africa, God gave me direction. I made it my goal to make other people's dreams come true. I would sit with our national church leadership and hear their vision. Then I would do everything possible to make it happen. I believe this is why I succeeded. I didn't come to South Africa with my own agenda but with a willingness to serve others and an attitude of love. God continues to expand this vision and grow His plan for my life.

My life's dream involves God's dream for Veniesha, Thabelo, Regaogetswe . . . the names could go on and on. If my life touches their lives and then their lives touch others, then the message of Jesus will reach the ends of the earth. It will reach the unreached. God has called me to raise up dreamers who will raise up other dreamers. He has called you to do the same.

> *Now to him who is able to do immeasurably more than all we ask or imagine, according to his power that is at work within us, to him be glory in the church and in Christ Jesus throughout all generations, forever and ever! Amen (Ephesians 3:20–21).*

God's fulfillment of the dream is more than we could ever ask or imagine. What are you doing to fulfill God's dream of making disciples who make disciples?

EPILOGUE
DREAMS DO COME TRUE

*"May the Lord answer you when you are in distress;
may the name of the God of Jacob protect you. May he
send you help from the sanctuary and grant you support
from Zion. May he remember all your sacrifices and
accept your burnt offerings. (Selah)
May he give you the desire of your heart and make all
your plans succeed. We will shout for joy when you are
victorious and will lift up our banners in the name of our
God. May the Lord grant all your requests."*
—Psalm 20:1–5

As a child, I dreamed of being a missionary and an author. For some reason, I thought I would have to wait until I was old before I shared my story in a book. In 2016, God encouraged me that the time to write this book was now, as a single woman serving as a missionary in South Africa.

This book holds all the lessons that God has taught me so far on my journey to know God and make Him known. I pray that it will help you draw closer to God and challenge you to share Him with others.

But there is one more story that I need to share. The Lord has answered my prayers. While I was in the process of writing this book, God sent me a future helpmate. God saw my years of sacrifice and obedience, and He granted me the desire of my heart.

I'm shouting for joy in the God who is faithful. At the right time, He gives us our unfulfilled dreams.

The man of my dreams is an ordained pastor from the USA. He loves missions and will join me on the mission field where we will serve God together.

My dream of being a "pastor's wife" came true after all.

The details of this new adventure are for another book. Only God knows the next chapters . . . for now.

ACKNOWLEDGMENTS

First of all, I want to give glory to God. His loving hand and favor have been upon me throughout the years. I'm thankful for His faithfulness and assurance on every step of life's Journey.

Secondly, I want to thank my family and friends for always being supportive of God's calling on my life.

I also want to express a special thank you to Mark Batterson for including me in his book *Chase the Lion*. That small paragraph motivated me to take the steps of faith to complete this book. When he chose to use my story, I realized that I had something to share that could impact others and encourage their faith.

Thank you to everyone on my "dream team": my prayer partners, financial supporters, fellow missionaries, and my national church body. You have all been a significant part of the work God has done and will continue to do.

My final acknowledgment is to you, the reader. You are part of this dream. My prayer is that this book has inspired you to "dream beyond yourself." When you put this into action, God's dream will be made real. For this, I am truly thankful.

DISCUSSION QUESTIONS

Introduction
Dream Beyond Yourself

1. Write down your life dream.

2. Discuss how today's culture is all about "me."

3. John 3:30. How can we make our lives less about "me" and more about God?

4. What dreams do you have for your life? Personal? Spiritual?

5. Psalm 37:4. How can my desires become God's desires?

6. How will your dream impact God's Kingdom and future generations?

7. Acts 9:3, 4–18. Have you had a Damascus road experience?

8. What else is God speaking to you?

CHALLENGE: Make sure your life is right with God. If you haven't yet, accept Jesus as the Lord and Savior of your life.

If you are studying this book as a group, take a group "selfie" and make a commitment to pray for one another throughout this study.

Chapter One:
The Milkman
(God's Dream)

1. What is God's dream?

2. As time allows, share the following testimonies in the group or break up into smaller groups of two

or three. Try to share your testimony in less than three minutes.

Have you experienced salvation? What is your testimony?

- **Before** you met Christ, what was your life like?
- **How** did you meet Christ?
- **After** you met Christ, how did your life change?

3. What is your testimony from this past week? What is God currently doing in your life?

4. What legacy did your parents leave you? What will you do to impact future generations? Is this similar to or different from what your parents did?

5. Acts 1:8. What is the purpose of the Baptism of the Holy Spirit?

6. Share about the last time you witnessed to someone.

7. Is everyone a missionary?

8. Matthew 28:19–20. What are we called to do?

9. How much time do you spend praying each day?

10. Will you commit to pray for missionaries and lost people? Write down specific names for your prayer list.

11. Do you attend a weekly prayer meeting? If not, how could you start or join one at your school, work, or church?

12. Is there anything holding you back from God's dream for your life?

13. Which action steps of faith will you take to move past your excuses and answer God's "calling"?

CHALLENGE: Pray for the Baptism of the Holy Spirit.

Chapter Two:
Shyness or Fear?
(God's Preparation)

1. Genesis 50:20. Talk about brokenness in your life's journey.

2. 2 Timothy 1:7. Tell about a time when fear stopped you from witnessing or sharing your faith.

3. How will you now be intentional in pushing beyond your comfort zone?

4. What obvious talents do you have? Have you discovered any talents that were hidden?

5. 1 Corinthians 12:4–6. How have you used your talents for God? How can you use your talents as an accountant, nurse, school teacher, or [insert your dream job here] to make God's dream come true?

6. Have you ever had to do something that was beyond what you thought you were capable of?

7. Look beyond the walls of your church. What are the needs in your community? How could you help meet those needs?

8. Luke 16:10; Colossians 3:23–24. If you take care of other people's dreams, then God will take care of your dreams. Can others trust you with their dreams? Are you faithful where God has planted you? List some other people's dreams that you can help accomplish.

9. Galatians 6:9. Are you tired or weary in doing good? Why or why not? What harvest will we receive?

10. Jeremiah 17:5, 7–8. What is the fruit of your life? Have your roots grown deep into streams of Living Water? Or are you trusting in your own strengths and abilities?

11. Will you dream beyond your natural abilities?

CHALLENGE: Pray for God to empower you with supernatural spiritual gifts.

Chapter Three:
Just Around the Corner
(God's Confirmation)

1. If you could do anything or go anywhere, what would you do?

2. Isaiah 6:8. How will you know what God's will for your life is? When He calls, will you obey?

3. Romans 8:14. Why do you need to be a believer to understand God's will?

4. Philippians 4:6; James 1:5. How does prayer help you understand God's will?

5. Romans 12:2; John 14:15. Why does the way you live affect understanding God's dream?

6. Psalm 119:105. Why should you study the Bible? Tell about a time when you were seeking direction from God, and the answer was confirmed in Scripture.

7. John 16:13. How has the Holy Spirit spoken to you in the past?

8. 1 Corinthians 16:8–9. How does God use circumstances to direct His people?

9. Proverbs 12:15, 24:6. Who has God used in your past to direct your life toward God's will? How do you feel about asking for advice?

10. Isaiah 42:16; Romans 10:14–15. What is God telling you? What is "just around your corner" that you may have neglected?

11. Acts 16:6–15. Is God redirecting your plan? If so, where is your Macedonia?

CHALLENGE: In the next week, pray and fast to seek God's confirmation for His will in your life.

Chapter Four:
Beggars
(God, My Provider)

1. Philippians 4:19. How has God provided for your needs?

2. Malachi 3:10. Do you tithe? If not, why not?

3. Philippians 4:15–16. Do you give to missions?

4. Acts 3:6–8; 1 Kings 17:7–16. Do you ask God in faith? What does that look like?

5. Luke 10:25–37. Tell about the last time you stopped and helped someone in need.

6. Luke 16:10. Can you be trusted with finances?

7. Matthew 6:21. Where does your money go every week?

8. Revelation 3:15–17. Are we like the church in Laodicea? Why or why not? What makes Jesus want to vomit? Who/what do you rely on to save you? How can your comforts cause you to be "lukewarm"? What steps will you take to be "hot" and not "cold" or "lukewarm"?

9. What does it mean to be blessed? What are you seeking more than anything else?

CHALLENGE: Take up an offering as a group or individually give to bless a missionary above what you normally do.

Chapter Five:
Strike!
(God, My Peace)

1. How much time each day do you spend on your cell phone, the internet, or watching TV and movies?

2. John 15:4–5, 9–11, 16. What does the word abide mean? How does a branch abide in the Vine? How do we abide in Jesus?

3. What does being "in love" with Jesus look like in your daily life?

4. 1 John 2:5–6. Are you obeying Jesus? In the past week, how often did you pray and read your Bible?

5. Luke 5:16. Do you make time to wait on Jesus? When was the last time?

6. Psalm 25:4–5. What are the benefits of waiting?

7. Luke 10:38–42. Are you a Martha or a Mary? Explain.

8. Exodus 20:8. Do you take a Sabbath rest? What should a Sabbath look like?

9. Romans 5:1; Isaiah 9:6b. Do you have high-stress moments? What does the peace of God look like in your life?

10. Summarize 1 Kings 17–19. Talk about a time when you felt like a failure. How does God care for us in an understanding and caring way (like He cared for Elijah)?

11. Are you willing to "strike" your current life? What needs to be changed in your life? Are there bad habits you need to break? Do you need to take some time off to seek the Lord for an answer?

12. What do you do when you have a bad day? How does worshipping God change your situation?

13. John 4:23. What does true worship look like in your life?

14. Close this chapter by singing a worship song.

CHALLENGE: Fast from media for several days and spend that time with God.

Chapter Six:
Ladybugs
(God, My Father)

1. Tell about a time when you felt like your dream crashed or got stuck in the mud.

2. What was your relationship with your earthly father like when you were growing up? How is your heavenly Father similar or different from your earthly father?

3. What do you need to ask your heavenly Father to teach you?

4. Acts 27:21–26, 33–37, 41; 28:1–10. How will you be like Paul and use your trials as platforms to proclaim your Father's love?

5. Are you willing to do whatever it takes to see God's dream fulfilled? What may be asked of you?

6. Psalm 121:1–2, 7–8. How has your heavenly Father helped you?

7. James 1:2–4. What can you learn through hardship?

8. Hebrews 12:7, 11. What can you learn from past mistakes?

9. What adventure does your Father desire to go on with you?

CHALLENGE: If your earthly father is still alive, tell him that you love him.

Chapter Seven:
Vampires
(God, My Defender)

1. Ephesians 6:12. Who is our battle with?

2. Exodus 14:14. What battles with the Enemy have you faced? How has God fought for you?

3. Acts 19:15. What do you think is the Devil's opinion of you?

4. 1 Peter 5:8. How does our culture allow Satan to devour it?

5. Luke 15:8. Is there any area of your life where you may be allowing the Devil entrance? What will you do to find what was lost?

6. 1 John 4:4; Revelation 12:11. Why should you not fear the Enemy?

7. Mark 4:35–40. What are the benefits of going through a storm?

8. 1 Corinthians 10:13; James 1:2–4, 12–13. What is the difference between a trial and temptation?

9. Romans 10:14–15. Even when the Enemy attacks, what do you do to make your feet "beautiful"?

10. What legacy are you leaving the next generation? What values will you instill in their lives?

CHALLENGE: Clean out your house. Do you have movies, magazines, books, music, pornography, alcohol, drugs, or anything else that is letting the Devil win in your life? If so, throw it out!

Chapter Eight:
Warts and Jawbones
(God, My Healer)

1. Isaiah 53:4–5; Psalm 103:2–3. Share about a time when God healed you.

2. Hebrews 11:1. What is faith?

3. Luke 1:37; 17:6; 18:1–8; Mark 9:24; James 5:14–18; 1 John 5:14–15. What steps do we need to take to be healed?

4. Job 2:7. If God cares so much then why does He allow sickness?

5. John 9:3; 11:4; Jeremiah 29:11. Why would He allow the righteous to suffer? How can the work of God be displayed in your life?

6. Romans 8:11. What is the Holy Spirit's role?

7. Luke 17:14. When you pray, do you check to see if God answered your prayer? How will you act in faith?

8. John 11:6, 45. Talk about a time when God was silent in your life. How can your healing journey be used to save others?

9. Luke 4:18–19. How does this passage apply to your life as it did to Jesus'?

10. John 14:12; Mark 16:17a–18b. How does God want to use you?

11. Stop and pray for those who need healing right now.

CHALLENGE: Visit a sick family member, neighbor, or church member. Encourage them and pray the prayer of faith over them. Get permission from a hospital or an "old age" home to visit, share a word of encouragement, and pray for the sick.

Chapter Nine:
Never Alone
(Dream Teams)

1. Talk about a time when you felt alone.

2. What teams have you been a part of? How did your team work together?

3. Acts 13:13; 15:38. Was there a time when you were jealous of or upset with another team member? Explain. 2 Timothy 4:11. How did you overcome this?

4. What team(s) is God asking you to be a part of?

   - Philippians 1:3–6. What does being on the prayer team look like practically?
   - Philippians 4:15–16. What faith step will you take to begin giving as a financial partner?
   - Matthew 28:19–20. Will you go on a short-term mission trip for a few weeks, months, or years? Will you pray and consider going for a lifetime?

5. Matthew 28:20. Who is with you always? Acts 1:8. Who is the most important member of the team?

6. Matthew 24:14. What must happen before Christ returns? Why has it not been done?

7. Ephesians 3:16–4:3. What can you do to walk in unity with others?

8. What is the vision that moves your team forward? Are you inside the riverbanks of what God is doing?

9. How can your team work together to go far in the same direction? Are you willing to lay down *your* dream for *our* dream? What will that look like?

10. Matthew 9:38. Pray for the laborers in the harvest field.

CHALLENGE: Go on a mission trip. Seriously, it will change your life! Talk with your local church to find out what opportunities might be available. If you reside in the USA, check out http://wideopenmissions.org for more information.

Chapter Ten:
True Love Waited . . . and Waited . . . and Waited. . . . (Unfulfilled Dreams)

1. Do you have unfulfilled dreams? What are they?

2. Hebrews 10:35–36; Habakkuk 2:3. What is God's promise for those who wait and persevere? Are there any conditions to the promise?

3. 1 Samuel 1:10; Psalm 62:8. How has waiting on the dream drawn you closer to God?

4. 1 Samuel 1:17–18; Mark 11:24. What does God promise will happen after you have prayed?

5. Romans 8:28. How can God use your unfulfilled dream for His good?

6. 1 Samuel 1:1–20. How does your story relate to Hannah's?

7. What is God's "happily-ever-after" for you? Are you willing to live it out now?

8. 1 Timothy 4:12; 1 Peter 3:3–5. In what way is your life proclaiming "you and God"?

9. Psalm 37:3–7a. How do these verses apply to your situation?

10. 1 Thessalonians 5:16–18; Proverbs 3:6. What can you do while you wait?

11. Pray for one another. Pray for patience and endurance while you wait. Pray for the fulfillment of the dream.

CHALLENGE: Write out a prayer to God about your unfulfilled dreams. Put this in your journal or a safe place. Write today's date on it so that when God fulfills it, you can look back and see that God is faithful.

Chapter Eleven:
Just When You Thought You'd Figured It Out . . .
(Dreams on the Altar)

1. When you were growing up, what did you want to become? What is your current job description or role in life?

2. Luke 20:25; Genesis 1:27. How can we give back to God what is God's?

3. Luke 9:23. What does true discipleship look like?

4. Romans 12:1–2. Is there any area of your life that you haven't released to God?

5. Why does God move us out of our comfort zones?

6. Genesis 22:1–3; 22:9–13. Why would God give you a promise and then ask for it back? Why does God want us to let go of our dreams?

7. Genesis 16:1–2. Share a time when you made (or almost made) an "Ishmael."

8. Galatians 4:29. How will you allow your dream to be birthed by the Spirit and not by an ordinary way?

9. Luke 14:33. Proverbs 19:21. Philippians 1:6. Talk about life's seasons.

10. Are you prepared and ready for the fulfillment of the dream? Are you doing everything you know to do now? Are you willing to change and do something different if God asks?

11. Which "cookie" applies to your life right now? Why?

    - Cookie #1: All the darkness in the world cannot put out a single candle.
    - Cookie #2: You will step on the soil of many countries.
    - Cookie #3: All the effort you are making will ultimately pay off.
    - Cookie #4: All the answers you need are right there in front of you!
    - Cookie #5: Adventure is not outside; it is within.

12. Are your dreams too small? What would be a big dream for you?

13. Will you lay your dreams on the altar?

14. Spend time in prayer surrendering your dreams to God.

CHALLENGE: Delayed obedience is disobedience. If God has spoken something to you through this book, act on it.

Chapter Twelve:
The Big House
(Dreams Fulfilled)

1. Matthew 28:19–20. What are you currently doing to fulfill God's dream of making disciples who make disciples?

2. What does it mean to be a disciple of Christ? What does it look like practically?

3. How has Jesus transformed your life?

4. Mark 1:15–20. What "costs" might there be in following Jesus?

5. How are you working yourself out of a job?

6. What is the evidence of discipleship in your life?

    a. FRUIT (John 15:7–8): What fruit do you see? What effect do you have on other people?

    b. LOVE (John 13:34–35): How do you show love to others in your daily life?

    c. SACRIFICE (Luke 14:33): Are you really willing to give it all up?

    d. COMMITMENT/OBEDIENCE (John 8:31–32): What are you currently committed to? Are you someone God can count on? Is your lack of commitment (disobedience) a disappointment to God and others?

    e. FISHER OF MEN (Matthew 4:19): How will you fish for people? What are you doing to introduce others to Christ?

7. Who are your friends?

   a. 2 Corinthians 6:14; Proverbs 27:17. Why should other believers be your closest friends?

   b. Matthew 11:19. Why should you be a friend of sinners?

   c. 1 Corinthians 15:33. Why might you need to let go of some friends?

8. Pray for God's dream to be fulfilled.

CHALLENGE: Choose a "Timothy" to disciple this next year and make an appointment to meet with them in the following week.

ABOUT THE AUTHOR

Sarah Careins grew up in the cornfields of rural Indiana, USA. From her childhood until the present day, she has always felt God leading her to impact the world for Jesus Christ.

She attended and volunteered at Master's Commission (a school of ministry and discipleship) where she gained hands-on experience in all types of ministry. She received her Ministerial Studies diploma through Global University in 2006 and was ordained as a minister of the Assemblies of God in 2008.

Sarah has served on the mission field since 2007. In South Africa, she helped relaunch and develop the National Youth Ministries of the International Assemblies of God and pioneered a university ministry, The Journey.

An accomplished speaker and writer, Sarah is most comfortable with the title of "disciple maker." She considers the development and training of young men and women for ministry one of her greatest passions and her calling.

In August 2017, Sarah married the man of her dreams—Russ. Russ is a graduate of Southwestern Assemblies of God University and an assistant pastor. He has a powerful testimony, evangelistic spirit, and a call to international ministry.

Russ and Sarah currently reside in Texas where they are preparing to return to the mission field together. Both believe that God will use them as a Spirit-empowered team to reach the unreached and train other disciple makers for God's dream.

Connect at www.sarahcareins.com.

ENDNOTES

1. I originally heard this on one of Mark Batterson's podcasts (www.theaterchurch.com). Unfortunately, I can't remember which one.

2. Ibid.

3. Center for Evangelism and Discipleship. *21st Century Discipleship Book 2: Facing Issues*. Springfield, MO: Global University, 2008.

4. *Urban Tribes*. Africa Assemblies of God World Missions. <urbantribes.tv>. Accessed April 3, 2017.

5. Comfort, Ray. "Hell's Best Kept Secret." *Livingwaters. com*. Living Waters Publications. <livingwaters.com/pdf/HellsBestKeptSecret.pdf>. Accessed April 6, 2017. This message was first preached in August 1982.

6. "Vampire." *Wikipedia*. Wikimedia Foundation, March 29, 2017. <en.wikipedia.org/wiki/Vampire>. Accessed February 16, 2007.

7. Stephens, Beth. "Lost and Found: A Personal Loss." https://bethstephens.org. I heard this message preached in 2013 on an audio CD.

8. "Never doubt in the dark what God told you in the light" quotation from V. Raymond Edman.

9. Plymire, David. *High Adventure in Tibet*. Springfield, MO: Gospel House, 1983. Page 83.

10. Smith, Oswald J. *The Cry of the World*. Valenzuela City, Philippines: ICI Ministries, 2008. Pages 58–63.

11. Joshua Project. <https://joshuaproject.net>. Accessed November 10, 2017.

12. Smith, Oswald J. *The Cry of the World*. Valenzuela City, Philippines: ICI Ministries, 2008. Page 64.

13. Waller, John. "While I'm Waiting." *Album: While I'm Waiting*. Reunion Records, 2009.

14. Elliot, Elisabeth. *Passion and Purity*. Grand Rapids, MI: Revell, 1984. Page 113.

15. Ibid. Pages 56, 60.

16. Vu, Michelle A. "VeggieTales Creator: Bankruptcy Humbled Me, Killed My Idol." The Christian Post. *The Christian Post*, May 6, 2011. <christianpost.com/news/veggietales-creator-bankruptcy-humbled-me-killed-my-idol-50119/>. Accessed February 1, 2017.

17. Sanders, J. Oswald. *Spiritual Discipleship*. Chicago, IL: Moody, 1994. Pages 7–9.

18. Similar quotations are attributed both to Dietrich Bonhoeffer and Billy Graham.

19. Name changed.